JOBS FOR
English Majors
and Other
SMART
PEOPLE

JOBS FOR
English Majors
and Other
SMART
PEOPLE

Revised Edition

John L. Munschauer
Director Emeritus
Cornell University Career Center

Peterson's Guides
Princeton, New Jersey

Library of Congress Cataloging in Publication Data

Munschauer, John L., 1919–
    Jobs for English majors and other smart people.
    Revised edition.

    Bibliography: p.
    1. Job hunting. 2. College graduates—Employment.
I. Title.
HF5382.7.M86   1986   650.1'4   85-31006
ISBN 0-87866-391-6

Composition and design by Peterson's Guides

Illustrations by John Huehnergarth

Printed in the United States of America

10 9 8 7 6 5 4 3 2 1

For information about other Peterson's publications, please see the
listing at the back of this book.

Contents

Why employers have a hard time evaluating candidates.
Interviewing—the imperfect courtship.

Rejection in the job market—a mismatch problem. The
two types of work and the one that is best for English
majors and other generalists. Types of employers and
employment.

Matching wits with skilled interviewers. "Tell me
about yourself. . . ." What you have to know to
respond intelligently. Questions you should and
should not ask. Howard Carroll learns first lessons in
interviewing.

What is really on employers' minds? How to get them
to see you as the answer to their needs.

Tried-and-true methods and how well they work.
Howard Carroll out on the street. Brunner Wengen's
doleful saga.

The hidden job market. Information interviewing; a
marketing strategy for uncovering opportunities.
Howard Carroll learns the technique.

Contents

Dedication

To: Stephen, graduate of the University of California at Berkeley, former hamburger chef in San Francisco, now a corporation lawyer;

Lynne, also a California graduate (U.C., San Diego), who has the bucolic life she always wanted as homemaker and mother, but is back in college taking education courses, looking to the future.

Amy, B.A., Middlebury College, mother and apiculturist;

Susan, riding instructor via Meredith Manor School of Horsemanship as well as builder of her own home (along with her husband), mother, and minimal contributor to the IRS by using the sun, the soil, and the forest to provide food and warmth;

Tom, who might have turned to music following graduation from Cornell but opted to break up atoms to find out about quarks and gluons;

Marg, linguist and Smith College's most peripatetic graduate, who finds such jobs as consulting for British Broadcasting in India or gets grants to study Urdu in Pakistan; and

Greg and Bruce, Macalester College and Albion students, respectively, the latest to bring home the question, "What can I do when I graduate?" For Greg the answer is getting a Ph.D. in chemistry; for Bruce it's cutting his teeth in the business world by selling insurance.

Preface
You Are the Reason for This Book

Tomorrow.

More job hunters.

Men and women searching for worthwhile careers.

You!

Your age? 17? 77? That's the age range of job hunters whom I have counseled over the past three decades, helping them choose and land the job they want. I want you to meet these people to learn of the ideas and strategies that brought them success. I want you to know how they failed at times. Unfortunately, we learn from failures; better theirs than yours.

Of course I can't have you meet all these job hunters because there have been thousands, but through fiction I can create characters and incidents that embody the essence of these people and their experiences. Also, through fiction I won't invade anyone's privacy. Yet I wish I could reveal identities to give credit where credit is due for their "how-to" suggestions.

But let's look at tomorrow. Five appointments. Men and women searching for worthwhile careers.

9 A.M. A liberal arts student without the vaguest idea of what he wants to do. He wonders what good it does to be an English major.

10 A.M. An experienced person out of a job—it happens all too often in the 1980s. High-tech companies expand in January and go broke in April. Mergers make people redundant. My client's company is closing because of foreign competition. Everyone says it's happening all over town, that there are no jobs to be had. "Everyone" could be wrong, but how to find employers who are prospering despite the times?

11 A.M.	A young woman who needs to revise her résumé. Her first draft was a "me" document, an obituary, not a document that speaks to an employer's needs.
1 P.M.	A housewife, college educated, who wants to start a second career now that her children are in school. She is discouraged because she can't even get interviews.
2 P.M.	You.

The English major is having career problems because he has asked the wrong questions. I must help him ask different questions so he can discover that there are more and varied openings for liberal arts graduates than for students with technical degrees. But I need more than an hour with him.

The person with experience is making the rounds of personnel offices and employment agencies as well as checking the ads. He may *never* find a job that way. There are many more productive and imaginative things he could do, but I can't begin to cover them in an hour. I need more time!

The woman with the résumé needs to see it from a new perspective. Résumés have become a cliché. We need to develop a different résumé and integrate it with a planned job campaign. That will take more than an hour.

The discouraged housewife. For over a year, she has been presenting herself to employers as a housewife and finding that no one except a husband needs a housewife. What employers do need is the rare person who can get things done. If she has gotten things done as a housewife, she can do the same as an employee. I want her to learn how to make employers see her as the capable person she is.

I have written this book for her, you, and everyone who needs a fresh way to look at the job search. No single thing is the key to finding and landing a job. Not résumés nor facile answers for interviewers, nor taking the right college courses, nor having a list of job openings ensures success. But there are principles of successful job hunting that will help everyone, and I want to show you how to use them in your own situation—no matter what it is.

The Changing Job Scene

Job prospects and career outlooks have changed drastically in the past few years. They promise to change even more. In fact, they are changing right now—for better and for worse, depending on your ability to understand what is happening.

Worse—   if you fall for the illusion that college graduates are sure to land jobs automatically. During the two decades of high employment following World War II and the Korean War, that may have been true. Besides swarming over the college campuses to recruit warm bodies, recruiters blitzed big cities, stealing experienced talent from other employers. Now, although recruiting on college campuses appears to be especially frenetic, scrutiny shows that it is concentrated on specialists such as engineers or, in the case of English majors and other generalists, on the cream of the graduating classes who are snapped up into management development programs. Most job hunters are left out.

Better—   if you can see beyond traditional recruiting to other kinds of employment opportunities.

Worse—   if you think that sending out résumés and filling out sterile application forms in employment offices are the ways to look for a job.

Better—   if you master the job-hunting techniques described in this book.

Worse—   if you were tracked in college to a profession that may eventually lead down the path of obsolescence. You've been trained to recognize only one kind of work, while really there are two.

Better—   if you learn about the second kind of work and all the possibilities it offers for a new and fruitful career.

Worst of all—if you suffer from ego/career paralysis, which is caused by an overemphasis on self-analysis aggravated by an overdose of career education. Career paralytics dwell on what they want in a career instead of looking for a way to apply their abilities in the real world of work.

Learn the Language of Employment

When you try to figure out what you can do, you may discover that your mind has been programmed to seek the answer in your educational preparation, rather than in the marketplace. You talk to yourself in the language of the educational monastery, not in the language of the employment marketplace. You may even talk yourself out of real jobs you would succeed at—and like.

This condition of poor communication is widespread. We are only beginning to realize its seriousness. When there was a shortage of talent, employers were willing to use the language of the educational monastery, but now, with supply and demand on their side, they no longer need to, nor do they try. They want to hear from candidates who speak their language. Those who learn it get jobs. Those who don't usually find themselves immobilized and confused, unable to figure out what to do except to go back to the monastery for still more education, which may only get them in deeper trouble.

I have searched in vain for a book about job hunting and career planning that translates the language of job hunters into that of employers. It isn't that the words employers use are different, it's that they are spoken from a different point of view. The very word "employment" means one thing to job hunters and something else to employers. Up to now, books on careers have been written in the language of job hunters, but it is time for a translation, and this is what I have attempted to write. *The result is a book completely different from anything you have read before on careers and jobs.*

In developing this translation, I have had to delve into the makeup of both job hunters and employment. While doing it, I learned something. There is not just one kind of employment—there are three; and there are two kinds of work. These discoveries do for job hunting what the discovery of blood types did for transfusions. They help explain why some types fit together and others do not. This book sorts out the types of work and employment, then tells you how to puzzle out which types of employment (or employers) are best for you. If, for instance, you are a liberal arts graduate, you will be pleasantly surprised to find you are like someone with O positive blood—you have the widest variety of possible "fits."

"Ah," say the vocational psychologists, "you are doing matching, which is what we do." Not really. The psychologist tells you to look into a mirror to see yourself, and thus to understand what you want and why. There is value in doing that, but you won't uncover jobs that way. I would have you turn the mirror to reflect the world of work, to see all the many interesting jobs there are. Only when you have taken a good look would I have you step into the picture.

Mine is a marketing approach, not a psychological one. An auto company, after a study of the market, aims its advertising for sports cars toward singles while it tempts families with station wagons. Similarly, your résumés, letters, interviews, and entire job campaign should be planned as if employers were consumers. This book, with its marketing approach, provides the key to helping you develop a job-hunting strategy that will give you a tremendous advantage in the job market. At the same time, it offers you the best chance of finding a job that suits you well.

The Ultimate Goal

My goal, then, is to help you find what historian Jacques Barzun calls True Work. True Work, he says, is "that which engages the heart and the mind, as well as the hand. It has a beginning and an ending. It is the overcoming of a difficulty one thinks important, for the sake of results one thinks valuable."

Acknowledgments

Fortunately, Ann Pitkin worked for me as an editor and saw the possibility of developing a book from my writing. That her father, Walter Pitkin, happened to be a literary agent was a further bit of luck. I found myself one evening discussing writing and job hunting with the two of them, and from that discussion this book was conceived. That meeting was only the beginning. In addition to becoming my agent, Walter became my mentor, adviser, and source of ideas. I thank him for his patience and willingness to stick with me in what I am sure turned out to be more work than he intended to put into this project.

I was equally fortunate in meeting Michael Twomey, now an English professor at Ithaca College. Michael read the manuscript and saw in it valuable ideas and, seeing that it was a bit like a ship under sail without a rudder, gave it the rudder it needed.

Mike Brush, as a journalist, edited some of my early work. From him I learned the value of a good editor. This lesson was again emphasized to me when my editors at Peterson's Guides put this book and its revision into final form.

I owe a debt of gratitude to certain executives at the Du Pont Company, as well as at Ford Motor, the National Security Agency, IBM, Federated Department Stores, Goodyear Tire and Rubber Company, the U.S. Bureau of the Budget and Management, Travelers Insurance, and the hundreds of other employers who invited me to observe operation of their organizations, to talk to their personnel, and even on occasion to travel with salesmen. Much of what I learned from this "show and tell" experience gave me the insight I needed to write this book.

Introduction

Listen to the Language of Employers

What goes through employers' minds during or after an interview? Let's listen to two business partners review an interview.

"You decide. Do we or don't we make an offer to Bollingbrook?"

"Thanks for handing the decision to me. I don't know. We really need someone who has more experience than a fresh college graduate, but judging from his summer house-painting business, he might have the maturity we need. Did you ever see his crew work? He had them working harder than Japanese in a Toyota factory. I wish we could get this business running half as smoothly. But when I talk to him, we don't speak the same language. He keeps talking about opportunity and challenge. 'Where will I be ten years from now?' he wants to know. Does he think we are going to put him on a track to his future? I keep telling him we have all kinds of things that need doing, and if he can do them there is no end to the responsibilities we can give him. Where did he get this hangup about opportunities? It is such a cliché."

"You know where. He is a college senior, and he is being fed that line by employers like G & P that recruit on campus. Speaking of clichés, your line about filling a need probably sounds like one to him."

"Probably, but don't put down G & P. Going with them for my first job was the best thing that ever happened to me. They do put you on a track, but it is a fast track, and keeping up with it is a challenge. How's that for a cliché? But it's true. Bollingbrook would do well to cut his teeth with them. Maybe he will; then when he's trained, let's see if we can try to lure him over to us."

"*If! If* he could get a job with G & P. *If* we could lure him over later. Too many ifs. Besides, I don't think he could get a job with them, judging from the way he handles himself in an interview. But what about trying to steal some talent from companies like G & P? We need seasoned, trained people more than we need raw talent."

"And how do we do that? Look what happened when we tried. Candidates didn't seem to understand that we were hiring because of our needs, not to promote their careers. Talk about clichés, by comparison, Bollingbrook is pithy. If we ever advertise to get applicants again, I am going to state that any applicant who describes himself as results or profit oriented or uses even one adjective or adverb in praise of himself will be rejected immediately."

"We won't get any applicants."

"Good. We won't have to waste time interviewing candidates we wouldn't consider anyway."

"Isn't it ironic? Four years ago you interviewed me for a job at G & P and practically threw me out the door when you learned I had a Ph.D. in English. What's more, do you know what you did when I tried to tell you that the diligence and intelligence I showed in getting my degree were talents transferable to your business? You yawned. Three nights later at our single-parents group, there you were, big as life, a new member. But when I told the group about the games and toys I had invented to keep the kids busy in the back seat of the car so I could drive in peace in the front, over you bounded to tell me how clever I was. You phony. You didn't even remember that you had interviewed me three days before. I almost turned away until I realized you wanted to talk about starting a company to market my inventions."

"Stop complaining. You're the president of the company now. You're getting rich. But tell me, would you hire a Ph.D. if one came knocking on our door and approached you the way you did me?"

"Probably not. Employment interviewing tends to bring out the negative. Instead of closing the gap between candidate and employer, it widens it."

"It isn't a gap, it's a Rubicon of our own making. But let's get back to my question. Do we or do we not make an offer to Bollingbrook?"

"I'll decide tomorrow."

"When?"

"Between brushing my teeth and making breakfast."

Interviewing vs. Communicating

What is going on here? Here are two people in business together who, when they met as applicant and employer, couldn't communicate, yet quickly got together when they found a mutual interest. Now as employers running a business they have interviewed Bollingbrook, and again there has been no communication. Could it be that there is a better way to discuss employment than through traditional interviewing? (There is such a way, but that is a story to be told later on.) Meanwhile, traditional questions and attitudes aren't proving productive for him.

Bollingbrook can't communicate with employers because his attitude is wrong. He is focusing on what he wants rather than on what his potential employers want. His problem is not unlike that of General Motors. If you ask executives in that company why it is in business, they will tell you it is to make a profit. But have you or anyone you've ever known bought a car because GM wanted to make a profit? You buy a car for two reasons: It fills a need and you like it. Bollingbrook will have to be shown that he will be hired when he fills a need.

Why You Will Be Hired

You will be hired for the same reasons—when you are liked and are seen as filling a need. Not that profit is to be ignored by you or General Motors. Without it GM will go out of business, and you won't be able to keep the wolf away from your door. Your challenge in job hunting, therefore, is just like General Motors': to find a customer with a need you can fill.

If Bollingbrook can be made to think of employers in terms of their needs as well as his own profit then he will begin to communicate with them in their language. More important, instead of just trying to sell himself in a routine canvass of personnel offices, he will conduct market research to find employers with needs he *can* fill and then devise a strategy for meeting and selling himself to appropriate employers. He will develop a prospect list of organizations that are growing and likely to be hiring. In other words, he will market himself.

This book will help you market yourself. It is based on eleven principles that are easy to learn, yet often hard to put into practice. Job hunting and the search for a career are so entwined in self-concepts and personal wants that the notion of serving a customer doesn't stay in the brain easily. Yet it must become part of the way you think, because the concept of marketing, of finding a need you can fill, is the key to successful job hunting.

Chapter 1

Planning Your Strategy

Analyze the job market to identify the type of work and the type of employer to seek.

To find a job, concentrate on employers whose needs match the type of person you are.

This principle may seem about as obvious as saying that to give a blood transfusion you have to match blood types. The catch is in knowing how to type blood, for a mismatch can cause a rejection. Similarly, faulty typing and matching in job hunting can cause another kind of rejection, the most common symptoms of which are:

- Complaints by new college graduates that employers are only hiring people with experience.

- Complaints from people with experience that employers want graduates just out of college.
- Overqualification problems.
- Feelings that one's education is useless.
- Feelings of being unwanted—especially common among older workers and women seeking a second career after completing the job of raising children.
- Visual problems—seeing only a fraction of the opportunities.

Typing often begins with trying to match a person's degree or experience with a label that has been placed on a job. A degree in engineering matches a job in engineering. People with sales experience are typed for jobs as sales representatives. Yet many of these may have qualities that better equip them for administration or research. That isn't typing, it's stereotyping. We might examine the way a woman raised her family and find that she is a superb manager, but do we call her a manager? No, we stereotype her with the label "housewife." Then, so labeled, she enters the job market, where her résumé is sent to employers who need people with management capabilities. What happens? *Rejection!*

She is not alone in her plight. Ask inventive engineers what happens when their specialty becomes technically obsolete. For example, what happens to vacuum-tube engineers when transistors replace most tubes? Is their inventiveness eagerly sought? Vacuum-tube engineers are seen by employers as vacuum-tube engineers. *Rejection!*

Ask Ph.D.'s in the humanities about their prospects of applying their fertile minds to business problems. Businessmen see them as teachers. *Rejection!*

But the loudest lament of all can be heard from thousands of voices in the liberal arts colleges whose rejection response goes like this:

How can I use my history major?
Oh, what's the good of philosophy?
Tell me what to do with psychology,
And what about anthropology?

No one answers their lament satisfactorily. Their attempts to find a match by asking, "What can I do with my major?" lead nowhere. It's the wrong question because it puts the cart before the horse. College degrees don't create work, needs do. Medical schools don't create the need for doctors, the need to be cured of an illness does.

For answers to questions about careers, begin at the beginning. Look to the world of work. Look at jobs to find out what needs to be done and how it is done. The question to ask is, "What do people do and what talents do they need to do it?"

TYPES OF WORK

An investigation of work reveals two types: professional and trait oriented.

Professional Work

In a profession, school-learned knowledge is applied to work. Surgeons learn anatomy in the classroom and remember what they have learned as they operate (patients hope). Engineers have a profession, as do college professors. They apply school-learned knowledge in their work.

Trait-Oriented Work

In contrast to professional work, there is trait-oriented work. In such work you apply yourself, your human traits, such as imagination or analytical abilities, rather than a school-learned skill. A banker has a trait-oriented job. In approving a loan a banker applies judgment, and judgment, unlike a knowledge of accounting or the law, cannot be taught in school. Nor can ingenuity, shrewdness, intelligence, persuasiveness, or any of the traits that are the essence of many occupations.

To find opportunities that do not require professional knowledge, listen to the language of employers. Listen for the words, "I need." You will hear advertising executives who speak of the need for people who can write creative copy, newspaper publishers who need to find reporters who can cover an art show one week and an economics conference another, or manufacturers who need people who can supervise labor. These employers all seek candidates who are competent, willing to work hard, and smart. As the hotel-owner who had originally set out to hire a trained hotel-school graduate put it when he chose a liberal arts graduate instead, "I needed a food and beverage control manager. I knew I could teach a smart person the job in a couple of weeks, and a liberal arts graduate convinced me she was smart."

7

TYPES OF EMPLOYMENT

Somewhere in the world of work there is an employer who needs you. An employer may be hunting for you as hard as you are hunting for him, but you may have to blaze your own trail. The tasks you face as a job hunter are beginning to unfold. One of the first things you must do is type, or classify, employers and employment to determine the best paths to follow to get you where you want to go. As an aid to orderly thinking, you might find it useful to divide employers or employment into these categories:

Type A: The Meritocracy
Type B: American Traditional
Type C: Do-It-Yourself

Type A Employment: The Meritocracy

You should know about the meritocracy. As a student you were in it. You may still be in it if you work for an organization that promotes from within, based on merit. The meritocracy is a system of continuing selection and promotion that begins with schooling and continues into employment. To be in the meritocracy is like being on a track.

Let's assume you are on it. You got on it in kindergarten where you played with the kinds of toys that helped develop an IQ that warranted placement in grade school on a track that led to a college-preparatory program in secondary school. Your achievement continued to be meritorious, prompting college admissions directors to solicit your application. You won acceptance at the college of your choice. Upon completion of your education, just as admissions directors had solicited your application previously, recruiters invited you to apply for jobs, and on the basis of merit you were one of the elite selected for a management development program. Your employer monitored your performance throughout your career and always found it meritorious. You moved up: salesman (Or was it administrative trainee? Both were beginning positions on your employer's track.) to manager, manager to vice-president, vice-president to executive vice-president, and on—straight to the top!

Is this you? If so, congratulations! You may one day be elected chairman of a company such as AT&T. I like what I see of merit organizations. Their managers try hard to select talent best suited to their needs. In initial assignments, graduates start in stimulating jobs where they can prove their mettle and be marked for promotion. Merit organizations pay well. If there is such a thing as security, merit employers offer it to the meritorious. And there are subjective benefits. People who work for IBM carry a certain aura of distinction beyond their pinstripe suits. Other people see them as smart. Merit employers confer prestige. For the right type of person, merit employers offer careers, not just jobs.

Merit employers do not hide their virtues under a bushel basket. Through advertising, by publishing attractive career brochures, and by campus recruiting, they do everything possible to entice job applicants, even locating company facilities in attractive parts of the country. The plan of merit employers is to attract a talent pool from which to select the best and the brightest. The meritocracy is selective, even elitist.

Merit Recruiting

Not all recruiting is merit recruiting. In engineering, where the supply is limited, even to fill routine engineering jobs, industrial firms must recruit. Not so for nontechnical positions. Nontech Incorporated can sit back and there will be no shortage of applicants knocking at the door of its employment office. But they can't count on this talent pool to include the brightest, the most motivated, and the most mature graduates. Merit companies may have combed the campuses and already identified and hired them. To be in the meritocracy, Nontech must recruit, or ivory-hunt as it used to be called.

Merit recruiting, however, even for the best and the brightest, is not quite the bonanza it seems. It is limited in scope. Banking is represented to some extent by the great metropolitan banks, as is merchandising by prominent retailers like Sears and Macy's. Procter and Gamble and other companies famous for their marketing skills recruit to ensure a supply of talent capable of helping them sustain their marketing leadership, while a few big insurance firms recruit for home-office administration, underwriting, and claims adjusting. Here and there an organization outside these industries will come up with something special, such as General Electric's business training program to feed smart people into its financial activities. While some states still have good merit programs to introduce bright young people into their civil service, the federal government hasn't had such a program for years.

Degrees as a Commodity—People as a Resource

Students tend to equate their degrees with jobs. This makes some sense in the professions, where employment prospects, like the sale of commodities, are determined somewhat by supply and demand. It should be noted, though, that engineers or accountants and some others with professional degrees don't have to place themselves at the mercy of recruiting. If they want to, they can always search out employers who need smart engineers or accountants, regardless of the apparent job market.

Liberal arts graduates must look for jobs that require smart people because there is no such thing as "liberal artsing," although students seem to think so at times. Possibly because recruiting notices and job listings are usually posted by degree in their college placement offices, students get conditioned to look for jobs as extensions of their degrees. That isn't smart. They don't see what there is to see. Let me illustrate by telling you how this book happened to get its title.

One day my editor mentioned that she once worked for the Princeton Placement Office. They would, she said, schedule a talk by a banker about banking or by a merchant about merchandising, and six or seven students would show up. When they saw what was happening, they invited others to speak about trait-oriented work and announced the talks as being about jobs for English majors; all the English majors showed up to learn about a wide variety of career possibilities. I picked up on the idea, hence the title *Jobs for English Majors and Other Smart People*.

The title was risky, but I felt it was a way to attract at least one group. Then, like dropping a stone in a pond and seeing the wave ripple out, the message might be passed on to others. Fortunately, it has worked that way. Now the goal of this edition is to drop the stone again to reach a wider range of new and old graduates in order to help them see themselves as more than commodities. To put it another way, this book is meant to help liberal arts graduates see themselves not as square pegs looking for square holes but as unique individuals capable of carving out a special place for themselves.

Why shouldn't an English major think of becoming a manufacturer? Why shouldn't an engineer interested in the environment use his knowledge as a lobbyist for a cause important to him? If someone wants to get into advertising, why pigeonhole her as an administrator just because her experience has been in administration? These people won't find merit employers out to recruit them. They will have to find their own jobs. They will have to look into American Traditional employment. Everyone should. You should.

Type B Employment: American Traditional

In the early part of the nineteenth century, Alexis de Tocqueville, the great French statesman, visited the United States to observe how a people free of the shackles of primogeniture and fixed social classes would order their lives and develop their careers. In his book *Democracy in America,*[1] he made this observation:

> In a democratic society, as well as elsewhere, there is only a certain number of great fortunes to be made; and as paths that lead to them are indiscriminately open to all, the progress of all must necessarily be slackened. As the candidates appear to be nearly alike, and as it is difficult to make a selection without infringing the principle of equality, which is the supreme law of democratic societies, the first idea which suggests itself is to make them all advance at the same rate and submit to the same trials. Thus, in proportion as men become more alike and the principle of equality is more peaceable and deeply infused into the institutions and manners of the country, the rules for advancement become more inflexible, advancement itself slower, the difficulty of arriving quickly at a certain height far greater.

He also observed:

> In an orderly and peaceable democracy like the United States, where men cannot enrich themselves by war, by public office or by political confiscation, the love of wealth drives them into business and manufacturing.

Were he alive today, Tocqueville might change the latter part of the sentence to "the love of wealth, the struggle for security, and the yearning for prestige drive them mainly to medicine, the law, or meritocratic employment."

Tocqueville would undoubtedly be interested in the way education has made possible the introduction of an elitist meritocracy without infringing on the principle of equality. But outside the meritocracy, would he find the paths to fortune all that different from those he had observed? We need to look at Wall Street, Bourbon Street, Market Street, and Mission Street, U.S.A. Big town or small town, these streets add up to Main Street, U.S.A. There one finds employment in the American tradition of Tocqueville—and at the same time vastly different. Different in that the paths to take are more numerous and varied, with education making it possible to travel on many of them at a faster pace. Entrée to these paths is secured by practices that developed through circumstance and became traditional. In the theater, young hopefuls park cars and take tickets at summer theaters, hoping for a break. In business, one young man follows his father into the presidency of a bank while

11

another works his way up from stock clerk to partner in an import-export firm. In politics, a volunteer in an election campaign eventually earns a position on a congressional staff.

Variety in Employment

Among the so-called traditional employers, you will find advertising agencies, brokerage firms, banks, film companies, circuses, cattle auctioneers, travel agencies, book clubs, consulting firms, food-processing companies, research laboratories, trucking companies, retailers, small manufacturers, and associations that send missionaries to the antipodes. If you would like to be with the Chicago Symphony Orchestra but don't have the talent to play, you should know that it is also an employer of administrators and people who deal with the public. If you could x-ray Main Street, U.S.A., you would see thousands of people doing interesting and important work, work they were able to master because they were well-educated, smart people.

Agencies, Contacts, and Nepotism

You may find a good job with a traditional employer through a help-wanted ad or an employment agency. So check these sources, but don't count on them. Most of the jobs won't be found that way. A lot of employment on Main Street happens because somebody knows somebody: An uncle hires his niece to get his sister off his back. (Nepotism is alive and well on Main Street.) Contacts can be very useful; take advantage of any you can. They will not guarantee you a job, but they will get you past the receptionist. More important in traditional employment, however, is being at the right place at the right time. This can, and often does, open up a job and does not require that you be anybody's relative.

Propinquity

An editor of a small-town newspaper, for example, may have the next edition all ready to put to bed except for the obituaries. But after twenty years of writing them, he is sick of it, especially today, because the sun is shining and he would like to be out playing golf. Then you, an aspiring journalist, happen along. You hit him at just the right time. You can do the obituaries. You have a job. Unfortunately, the editor, like most other traditional employers, has not hired you with an eye toward promoting you when a better job opens up. That would just reopen the obituary job, and the problem would have to be solved again.

You don't want a dead-end job, though, so you make sure the job won't be one. You become involved with the people in town. Soon you know all about them and their families. When someone dies, you don't just hack out a death notice, you write a bit of local history. Before long, your writing is noticed, and other papers want you. You are on your way in the American tradition.

It is not always easy for new college graduates to convince Main Street employers they are worthwhile job candidates. Many traditional employers like to fill their important positions by stealing talent from organizations that have reputations for developing talent. IBM in computers, Procter & Gamble in consumer products, and Abraham & Straus in department store merchandising are sometimes referred to as "academy employers" because of their ability to train talent. These companies pay a price for their excellence, though, because other employers try to lure away the people they have trained. A successful stint as a buyer for Abraham & Straus is worth more to a Main Street merchant than any M.B.A. degree.

If there is one single factor that differentiates traditional employment from the meritocracy, it is that in the latter you would be on a track that is not open indiscriminately to all. In traditional employment, there are all kinds of paths to success. You will have to discover them for yourself, and to do so you will have to master various important job-hunting techniques. Whether you will find the pace slow, as Tocqueville found it when the paths were traveled by people who did not have the advantage of an education, will depend in part on how well you use your educated brain. Some of you will find the best path by blazing your own trail, rather than following an established path.

Type C Employment: Do-It-Yourself

Peter Drucker, a well-known business philosopher, claims: "There is only one valid definition of a business purpose: to create a customer."

In do-it-yourself employment, it is the individual who creates the customer. An artist who paints a picture a buyer cannot resist creates a customer. An extraordinary singer or dancer, not the concert hall, entices us to buy a ticket. In another way, an insurance broker is a do-it-yourselfer. Insurance companies write the policies, but the broker finds people who need insurance and convinces them of the need.

Most do-it-yourselfers get where they are because they have had experience in another type of employment. For example, an industrial engineer who has worked for General Motors and developed a reputation as an expert in his field leaves the company to set himself up as a consultant. Salespeople, because they get around, often see a need that isn't being filled. A lumber salesperson who sees a need for a lumber yard for hardwoods starts a business to fill the need. An engineer in a research laboratory develops a servomechanism in his free time that manufacturers can't see the need for and won't produce, so the engineer forms his own company and makes a fortune manufacturing servomechanisms. My house was built by a college graduate who took a job as a carpenter because he liked to work with his hands. Now he has his own construction company, and I can't get him to build an addition to my house—his company has too big a backlog! He is building a profitable organization. From working for an organization, to becoming a do-it-yourselfer, to creating an organization of your own is a common pattern. If you would like to be your own boss, it is a good pattern to follow.

THE EMPLOYMENT MARKET

Drucker's notion of employer as customer applies to all three types of employment, indicating a need for market research to: (1) develop a list of potential customers and (2) determine how to market yourself to these customers. Is there an open market where jobs are listed? Are there other paths to employment such as internships or part-time work? If there is no job opening, what are the possibilities of developing one? What have others done to get their jobs?

One outcome of market research should be the development of a plan for a job campaign that divides the job market into categories as follows:

I. **The Open Market**
    A. **Type of employer**
        Meritocratic. A major criterion for selection of candidates is their growth potential.
        a. *Interviewing.* Initial screening, probably by a skilled interviewer, followed by interviews with those with whom you will work.

      b. *The Challenge.* To come across as a person with potential for advancement.

    American Traditional. The employer has a specific need, e.g., a sales representative. Advancement potential is probably secondary.

      a. *Interviewing.* Initial screening by a personnel department or immediately by the person for whom you may work. Interviewer will probably be amateurish.

      b. *The Challenge.* To show you can do the job and fit into the organization.

B. Listing agents
College placement offices, public and private employment services, advertisements, employment directories, and employers' personnel offices.

C. Marketing aids
Letters, résumés, portfolios, recommendations.

D. The market
Opinions vary. In general, experts estimate that no more than 30 percent of all jobs are filled through the open market.

II. The Hidden Market

A. Type of employer
American Traditional. Employers, especially those who are expanding, have unfulfilled needs that have not yet developed into a job listing or may not be apparent.

      a. *Interviewing.* The job hunter interviews the employer to ascertain needs.

      b. *The Challenge.* To uncover a need and sell your ability to fill it.

    Do-It-Yourself. Discover a need you can fill by creating your own business.

B. Prospecting for employment possibilities
Using directories and other aids to research the market. Developing a network of contacts who can provide information and introductions.

C. The market
Unlimited.

You have been reading about concepts to help you lay out a plan for pursuing your job hunt. To help you implement your plan, let me take you directly to employers and have you meet them face to face in interviews. In that setting, you can observe reality and then become more pragmatic in your approach to research. You can discover what is on the minds of employers and gain a better understanding of how to respond to them. Since interviewing will be an important part of your research, starting first with principles of interviewing does not necessarily put the cart before the horse.

Chapter 2

Speaking the Language of the Meritocracy

In an interview with the Meritocracy, you must be able to
answer questions in ways that reveal your growth potential
as well as your job skills.

What do you want from an employer? Security? Interesting work?
Make a list of your wants. You might as well try to get what you want.

What do you offer an employer? Experience? Training in a
profession such as engineering? Creativity? Again make a list. What
you offer an employer is what will get you employment.

Don't struggle too hard making the lists, because "I want" and "I offer" are words in *your* language. They make you think about yourself, whereas a true insight into employment comes from understanding the language of employers. Their language is, "We need." You must learn to speak that language when you look for jobs, but you will also find that learning about employers' needs is the best way to expand your own understanding of what you offer.

While "We need" is the universal language of employers, the meaning of words can vary from employer to employer just as it can vary from place to place. In England, when a play "bombs" it is a success; here, it is the opposite. The key word in the language of employment is "competence," but the way competence is understood varies according to the type of employer.

Traditional employers hire because they need someone to do a specific job; for them, competence is the ability to do that job. In the meritocracy, employers need people with growth potential; therefore, they see competence in terms of personal qualities. Not that useful talents are unimportant to them, but the success of an organization depends on leadership, and qualities of leadership are scarce and hard to find.

In the meritocracy, recruiting leadership requires a carefully planned strategy, such as that of Procter & Gamble (which, to its possible regret, has been selected here as the epitome of the meritocracy). Imagine a manpower chart of that organization as a pyramid stuck full of colored pins. At the top there is a pin for the president; beneath that, several more pins for the executive vice-president widen in the next row to more pins for the vice-presidents. Then, there are ever-widening rows for each level of manager, until finally the widest row of all, pins for the salespeople, engineers, marketing specialists, and others who occupy similar important but nonmanagerial positions. Pin colors indicate who will retire and when; experience tells how many will resign, die, or get fired. Attrition is planned for. As openings occur, Procter & Gamble could conceivably seek replacements from the outside, but as a leader in its field it knows that no one knows the business better than its own people. Therefore, it fills openings by moving people up the pyramid until the vacancies show up in the bottom row. That row, for Procter & Gamble, represents jobs that must be filled through recruiting. The positions are regarded as entry-level assignments and a training ground for future management.

If you are an engineer, for example, who would like to get into manufacturing with Procter & Gamble, put yourself in the shoes of the recruiter who will judge you as if you were two persons, one an engineer, the other a potential leader. The former judgment can be made largely by examining your college transcript; the latter must be made by interviewing you to assess your diligence, imagination, maturity, intelligence, physical vitality, temperament, and other traits that indicate your potential for growth. Your interview won't be too different from that of someone interested in a sales position, where traits indicate both aptitudes and growth potential.

Be prepared for an interview, whether you are an engineer or a language major. *The purpose of an interview is to find out what sort of person you are. This is what interviewing is all about.*

WHAT INTERVIEWERS WANT TO KNOW

What kind of a person are you? To find out, merit interviewers will ask you about yourself, about aspects of your life, about things you have done. A pattern of success and ambition in your life would indicate that you have the ability to succeed and grow. So they will ask:

Why did you go to college?

Did you earn all or part of your way through school?

What extracurricular activities did you participate in?

What did you do during your vacations?

Where have you been employed, and what did you do?

What do you want to do with your life? What are your goals?

What kind of a job interests you? What kind of work do you like to do?

What accomplishments are you most proud of?

The merit interviewers will want to know how mature you are and whether you have a positive attitude. To find out, they may ask:

What qualifications do you think you have that will make you successful?

What have your bosses been like? What kind of a person have you enjoyed most as a supervisor? As an associate?

What do you think will determine how well you will get ahead?

Did you enjoy school? Work?

What are your major weaknesses? Strengths?

Are you cooperative?

Do you seek attention?

What kind of people do you dislike?

The interviewers will also be likely to ask the following questions to find out about your loyalty and integrity:

What do you think of your last employer? Would you work for him or her again? Why, or why not?

What do you think determines success in a company?

Why do you want to work for this company?

What organizations have you belonged to? Have you held any offices in them?

The following questions are designed to learn about your work habits and some of the traits that might make you a valuable employee:

What have you done that shows imagination? Leadership? Initiative? Willingness to work?

Can you describe some of your accomplishments?

Do you mind working overtime?

What kind of work do you like to do the most? The least?

What do you know about our organization?

Why do you want to work for us?

Are you willing to travel?

All of these questions are typical of those asked by meritocracy interviewers. On paper they look trite, and spoken they frequently sound that way. You could cook up superficial answers that would get you past some recruiters, but don't count on getting away with that at Merit, Inc. You could quickly make a fool of yourself if one of their interviewers picked up a superficial answer and pressed like a lawyer with a witness who can be led to contradict himself. Remember, for a skilled interviewer, the questions are simply openers to get you to reveal yourself. So it's important that you know yourself, and that's not easy. Here's a device that should help: write an autobiography that includes the things you have done, so you can deal quickly with questions without fumbling. You won't be able to read from it during your interviews, but the exercise of writing the autobiography will prove a useful discipline to help you remember the really important things.

Write your autobiography in the language of employers. If you are interested in a job in design, advertising, or some other creative field, write up what you have done that illustrates your creativity. If the job requires analytical ability, put down on paper examples of what you have done that demonstrate that ability. What have you done that shows initiative? Energy? Perseverance? These matter to an employer. But don't panic if you are having trouble preparing such an autobiography at this point. The rest of the job-hunting principles we will be discussing will help you to understand the language of employment and to remember things you have done that have meaning in terms of employment.

If you have already been employed, you should not have too much trouble preparing an employment-oriented autobiography; but even if you have never worked for pay, you have worked. You have worked in school. You have worked at recreation and play. You have worked in family situations. In all of these activities you will find the answer to the two questions that are on the mind of every employer: (1) What *can* you do? (2) What *will* you do?

Past Actions—the Key to Future Performance

Don't be surprised to find your interviewer from Merit, Inc., probing your early background for the answers to those questions, even if you are a person with considerable experience. That early period in your life, interviewers feel, is where the pattern is set that determines the kind of person you will be. No matter how young or old you may be, there is a gold mine of information about you in your most ordinary experiences. A job hunter may tell an interviewer, "I haven't really done anything." But after some skillful probing, the interviewer may discover several things that the person did as a camp counselor, for example, that reveal qualities that any employer would be eager to have in an employee.

Interviewers, however, are not going to pull information from a reluctant interviewee. They may ask a question to give you a lead, feeling that one way to assess your abilities is to judge how well you present yourself. Put yourself in a recruiter's shoes and judge how well you come across. The recruiter's mission is to screen applicants and refer them to managers who will do the actual hiring. If, in an interview for a sales training program, you say you are unsure of your interest in sales but wonder about something in administration, the recruiter is going to be annoyed. He is exhausted from traveling around the country looking for people interested in sales, and you focus on an entirely different job area. What is he supposed to do? Report back to his manager and say, "I have a candidate, a very nice person, but I am not sure he wants to sell"?

If you were in the recruiter's shoes, you would not recommend such a candidate. Help the recruiters. They look long and hard for candidates who will be a credit to their judgment. What they want an interview to be is just what you want it to be—an exchange between two people sincerely trying to establish whether they have a mutual interest, with neither party trying to intimidate or manipulate the

21

other. The recruiters, however, are the questioners; if you are not prepared with answers, you are going to feel as if you were on trial.

PRACTICE INTERVIEWING

Let's take you through an interview and see how you do. Because the purpose of interviewing is to find out what you are like, let's create a scenario in which the job in question doesn't require any specialized training or experience. That way we can concentrate on an interview that is concerned almost entirely with personal qualities.

Meet Your Interviewer

You are to be interviewed for a bank job. Your interviewer is about 35. She was happy and successful as a loan officer, when her life was suddenly changed (for the worse, in her eyes): She was promoted from a pleasant job to one of the hardest and most baffling jobs of all—interviewing 22-year-olds in order to pick the ones who can become successful bankers.

You don't know it, but the president of the recruiter's bank cooked up a crafty scheme whereby up-and-coming executives were selected for advancement according to their ability to pick talent. Over a three-year period, your interviewer has to hire eight to ten college graduates per year as trainees for management positions, and her fate hangs on their rate of progress—or their failure. This is her second year of this work.

If you think you are nervous, you ought to be the interviewer. When she was selected for the honor of being a recruiter, the deal was supposed to include a three-week course on interviewing, but that fell through. Then a scheduled two-day session on the same subject at the American Management Association offices was canceled because of a blizzard. She has read a book on interviewing— and that is all the preparation she has had. (In that way, at least, she is not unlike a lot of other interviewers!)

Sweaty Palms

So here you are, the two of you, both nervous. You have a sweaty palm. Fortunately, before you shook hands you dried your hand, and that firm grip you gave her, along with looking her straight in the eye, covered up your anxiety. In fact, it made you feel quite confident. Secretly, with her stomach tied in knots, the banker wonders how she will handle the interview and wishes she had your composure. What should she say to you? She remembers the book. It says to break the ice with a few minutes of chitchat: the latest weather, last night's basketball game. Your conversation turns to the local airline, and you have a good laugh that relaxes you.

You are relaxed, that is. The banker is not. What should she say to you now? If only you were both engineers, then the two of you could talk about gears and motors, something impersonal that would make the conversation easier.

BE PREPARED TO TALK ABOUT YOURSELF

After a long pause, she turns to you and says, "Tell me about yourself." That dumps the whole load on you. How would you respond? Get out a piece of paper and write your answer now.

Of course I don't know how you will respond to this and subsequent questions, but if I can assume that you have just graduated from a liberal arts college, I have a basis for anticipating your responses. Liberal arts graduates constitute a model because they must sell themselves in the job market, although even if you are an engineer or someone with experience, when you cut through to the essence of an interview you must still sell yourself.

There are two ways to answer a question such as "Tell me about yourself." One takes a tack like this: "I was born in Buffalo, the son of parents who . . ." Another pursues this route: "To give you an insight into what I am like, let me tell you what I did last summer. I organized a business to paint stripes in shopping center parking lots. First I had to sell . . ."

Which tack did you take? Ask yourself whether your answer would help the employer see you in terms of what you can do for him.

In less than three sentences, the second candidate revealed organizational ability, imagination, ingenuity, and a talent for sales. Note that he did it by telling what he did. If he had said, "I have organizational ability, imagination, ingenuity, and a talent for sales," that answer would have been good *if, and only if, he had immediately backed it up with examples to prove his point.*

Because habits are set early in life, skilled interviewers probe for early experiences. This response also would go over well: "The best way to tell you about myself would be to tell you about my first job. Just as soon as I was old enough, I got a newspaper route, where I earned enough money to . . ." (It wouldn't hurt if the recruiter had once had a newspaper route.)

Tune Your Answer to the Job

If possible, tune your response to the job in question. If the bank listed a job in operations for someone with administrative, organizational, and leadership ability, could you think of something you have done to illustrate those qualities? If you were a team manager or a class officer in college, you might find that you could demonstrate the qualities you used in the job by telling how you handled it.

People who have worked for several years or more, whether in a salaried managerial position or in volunteer work, can draw on experiences to prove their competence. It is not as easy to relate educational experiences to employment, yet going to college is a job. Reports you wrote, and the grades you received, reveal competence. Interviewers have probably had to write many reports in their work, so reports are almost certainly something they can relate to.

An employer once hired somebody because she told him that in college she had a special basket for nasty little chores she could do in those dead times just before dinner, when it was not worth getting into a project that required long periods of concentration. He knew he would get a good day's work out of her when he hired her, and he did.

Younger job hunters must realize that their experiences as waiters and waitresses, door-to-door salesmen, and camp counselors can also be related to employers' needs. Most applicants seem to think that the only kind of job worth mentioning is something like a summer internship in the office of a senator. When you get to the part of this book that tells about letter writing and résumés, you will see how a summer job as a baby-sitter got a candidate a job in journalism!

Research the Job Before the Interview

Here comes the next question:
Why do you think you would like banking?
Before you answer, wait. It's a logical question, yet it may throw you off because you may never have had any banking experience except to open an account. If you have no basis for answering the question, don't try. Instead, write down how you would prepare yourself to answer such a question.

Good! You did have a basis for answering. You said:

I got interested in banking partially because banks are interested in me. Your bank and others advertise in the *College Placement Annual,* so I sent away for recruiting brochures and found the work most interesting. On page 16 of your brochure [as you talked, you had the booklet with you and opened it to that page], you described the duties of a loan officer as . . .

You won the recruiter over right there. Do you know why? You did it because you read the company's job description and brochure, and that alone set you apart from the crowd. The biggest single complaint from recruiters is that candidates don't read job descriptions or recruiting brochures.

Read

Just a simple thing like reading what there is to read may get you the job. It is amazing how candidates can spend four years in college knocking themselves out to pass tests and then won't spend ten minutes preparing for a lifetime career. Too many candidates go into interviews winging it, thinking recruiters will usher them into a career.

Investigate

Of course, if you really want to know why banking might be a good field for you, talk to bankers and learn what they do. You will find that in medium-sized cities bankers become very much a part of the community, perhaps just as you became a part of the campus by participating in activities. You will find that banking is a business in which one becomes deeply involved with people and their problems. Bankers become involved when they lend money to businesspeople to help them finance their ventures or when they mortgage a home for a young couple. If you show this extra interest, you would put yourself far ahead of other candidates. The recruiter won't meet many applicants who have looked into banking and who can give an informed reply to the question, "Why do you think you would like banking?" Let's assume that you further replied:

> After reading about banking, I looked into it. I visited four different banks and learned how bankers are involved in their communities— helping with the United Fund campaign, for example, or serving on the board of the local art gallery. In college I was active in campus affairs. The alumni secretary had me speak at reunions, and I was a vice-president of the Interfraternity Council. From what I could learn, some aspects of being a banker would be a straight-line continuation of the kinds of things I enjoyed doing on campus. I want to be a member of a community, and banking is one way to do it.
>
> Also, I was interested to learn how bankers get involved with their customers. I found out that when a banker makes a loan, he becomes a partner of sorts in the enterprise, and . . .

You have just made a tremendous impression! Do you know what you have done? You actually found out what the job was all about so you could talk sensibly about it. You really found out why you were suited for banking! It wasn't all that difficult to do, but it set you apart from the competition.

Chapter 2

Clarify Your Goals (to the Extent You Can)

Next question:

What are your future vocational plans?

Write down what you think you would say.

Oh, oh! If you answered that you hoped to go to graduate school in a few years to get an M.B.A., you flubbed it, because that means you are not interested in a long-term commitment. If you had read the brochure, you would have seen that the bank was hiring for the long run. You would have noticed that it has its own management development program in conjunction with the American Institute of Banking. You forgot one of the fundamentals of the language of employment, namely, that employers are going to interpret what you say in terms of, "What is this person going to do for me?" Your answer says, "I am going to use the bank for a couple of years, then just when they need the training they've given me I am going to leave and go back to school."

Questions about goals, long- and short-range plans, and the like are favorites of recruiters. One person, looking back on a highly successful job campaign that netted seven offers, made this comment about questions relating to goals and plans:

> When I was looking for a job, I was asked the same question in one way or another about a dozen times. I answered that I could not be that analytical about my goals and ambitions. I told them that I had always been a good student and that I enjoyed being with bright and active people. I did well in primary and secondary school and in college. When I did well, opportunities opened up for me. I told them that I hoped to get a job with a good employer and do my best there just as I had done in school, and that I expected further opportunities to open up, although specifically where or when I didn't know. I found what I wanted in education by working hard and contributing, and I expect more of the same at work. I do not worry about career goals.

It was a good answer, because in his case it was an honest answer.

A question about goals almost starts college students twitching these days, with parents, teachers, and counselors hounding students at an early age about their career plans: "What are you going to do when you graduate?" "A history major? How are you going to use that?" Careers, careers, careers. The words are drummed into dear little ears, and then into dear big ears, so that at long last when it is time to look for a job, candidates are practically paralyzed because they have not been able to see fifty years into the future with every move.

It is too bad that the tables can't be turned so that candidates could

26

ask their interviewers, "Tell me honestly, what were your goals in college, and did they mean anything? Has your life worked out according to a plan? Don't you think all of this business about goals is a bit stupid?"

Felix Frankfurter, the great Supreme Court Justice, once asked *Harvard Law Review* students and alumni, "Why did you study law?" Half the students and the top lawyers from the top law school in the country replied, "We did not know what else to do." So don't feel foolish if you can't reply to all the questions with the insight of a Freud.

If you have searched your soul and find that you seek neither the Holy Grail, nor gold in large amounts, nor power, nor fame, then could it be said that your goal is to grow by putting your roots down in fertile soil? Now *there's* an answer! (This is an effort to give you ideas, not phrases to parrot back to an employer; it could sound phony if you described yourself as a plant and an employer as soil. Just put it in your own words.) A student once picked up a similar idea and gave an answer that sounded perfectly natural: "I am looking for a job that will give me a good start and some momentum; then I will add my energy and move ahead on my own."

Know Your Strengths and Weaknesses

Brace yourself for the next question. It's a stinker.

What are your strengths and your weaknesses?

Again, write down your honest answers.

I presume you prepared an autobiography listing your accomplishments. Did you go a step further and determine the qualifications that can be attributed to your various successes? If you did, you have a list of your strengths. But what about your weaknesses? You may know them, but don't let the interviewer trap you into making a confession of something damning. Tell about your weaknesses, but put a twist on them to turn them into strengths. For example:

> I did not find college all that difficult, but I found that I could easily fall into poor work habits. In my sophomore year, my grades slipped when I goofed off because there was not enough to do. To correct this, I got into many activities that forced me to learn to use time effectively.

Here is a depersonalized response, because it avoids the danger of making a confession (and is also a good way to test employers' attitudes towards graduate study):

> My college offered only one course in accounting, and I think I should have more to do a good job in business. I want to make up

27

this deficiency. Do you have a program of further education to help employees get the courses they need to perform well?

You can also use the question to show what you got out of a liberal education, and that may be very good because many employers who didn't graduate from a liberal arts program don't know the benefits to be gained from such a curriculum. For example:

Writing has not been my strong point, but I took a course in the history of music because the professor required a term paper that demanded considerable research and would be graded not only for content but also for style and grammar. The professor had a reputation for being one of the toughest on campus, but I am glad I took the course because it did a lot for my writing and for my ability to organize ideas.

Or you might say:

I wish I had a better memory, but I have improved it by taking foreign languages. Nothing in college has done more for my mental discipline than the study of languages.

The question has traps, and many fall into them. Telling an interviewer that a course was taken because it was tough might be stretching the truth, and if so don't say it. Recruiters can spot phony answers. Keep answers simple and sincere. As one recruiter put it,

The way a question is answered is what interests me. Our company offers good jobs, and while we have carved out a nice niche for ourselves, we are a minor factor in our industry. When I ask candidates why they want to work for us, some start to give me a big line about what we are not—leaders, innovators, and so on. Others simply state that they are interested in the kind of work we offer, and I respect that. Then along come those rare candidates who state that they have looked into our company and found that while we do not innovate, we do produce quality products at a low cost, resulting in high profits. The first type of candidate I never hire, the second I might, and the third I always do. I made an offer recently to a woman who was so nervous that it took a while for her to tell her story—but she really knew what she was talking about.

Be Your Best Self

If you are a bit flamboyant, tone it down, although not to the point of false modesty. One job hunter I knew named O'Brian looked a recruiter straight in the eye and said, "As for my goals, they are to become president of your company in not too many years." The recruiter called him arrogant and told him to see a counselor. That same day O'Brian was asked again about his vocational plans by another recruiter and gave the same self-assured answer. This recruiter was delighted. As he said later, "All day long, I'd been asking students what they wanted to be in our company some day, and I'd been getting evasive or self-effacing answers. Then O'Brian came along. He is smart and knows what he is after. He is the candidate I want."

Now You Can Relax

Put your pencil down and relax. There won't be any more tough questions. You have made it through the first twenty-five minutes of a thirty-minute interview. You have answered the questions with sincerity and shown a clear interest in the job without sounding like a sycophant. In the remaining minutes, the banker will probably explain what you can expect from her. She may say that you will hear from her in two weeks (that usually means four) about any invitation for further interviews.

QUESTIONS YOU SHOULD AND SHOULD NOT ASK

At this point in an interview, a recruiter may ask if you have any questions. If the recruiting brochure does not cover initial job assignments, training, and other things you should know about, then ask about them. If you have no questions, a shrug and a listless "no" can leave a recruiter with a negative impression. Say something like, "Not that I can think of right now. The brochure (or the interview) covered the situation well. It gave a good picture of the career paths in your organization." One way or another, you ought to convey to recruiters that the give-and-take has been worthwhile for you. As it should have been.

Don't ask about vacations, pay, pensions, and working hours; don't give the impression that you are after a sinecure. Let employers make an offer first, then ask the "I want" questions. If they don't like them, it is harder for them to withdraw an offer than it is to withhold it in the first place. You *can* ask any recruiter what to expect if you are invited back for further interviews.

Make sure you have the recruiter's name and title; you should write a letter of thanks for the interview. You may also want to ask for, or give, further information.

With luck, you will be invited back to the company at its expense. Expense arrangements are usually made very clear in a letter of invitation, but if they are not, don't assume anything—ask.

At the company, you may be given some tests, although tests are now used less and less frequently. You will probably be interviewed by a few more people, possibly by the person who will be your immediate supervisor if you are hired. The visit should be a two-way street. You should be given a chance to see where you would work if hired and to meet some of the people with whom you would work. If you are not given that chance, ask for it. Candidates are also frequently given an opportunity to talk to trainees, who are likely to be candid about what the work is like.

There are certain questions the employment process should resolve. What are you like? What is the work like? Will you be good for the employer and the employer good for you? If the employer has mastered the art of interviewing, you will be halfway toward resolving them all. You can resolve the other half by learning the art of being interviewed. If you feel comfortable and competent in the interview you have just gone through, you may very well get a good job in the meritocracy. But you will have to be sharp, sharper than Howard Carroll, whose story needs to be told. You can learn from him.

The Case of Howard Carroll
Part 1: Light Begins to Dawn—
First Lessons in Interviewing

Howard Carroll, a typical senior in a large university, was interviewed for a training program by a recruiter from a large insurance company. Halfway through the interview, the interviewer, Frank Wetherbee, pushed aside his papers, leaned back in his chair, and paused while he contemplated the young man across from him. Howard squirmed, wondering what was coming. It was the first time he had ever been interviewed by a recruiter. He knew the interview with Wetherbee wasn't going well.

"Howard," the interviewer said, "you're a nice guy. I suspect you have a lot to offer, but I am going to be very blunt because I want to jolt you into changing your interview tactics. Based on the interview this far, we would not hire you even if you were the only person available.

"People in an interview," he went on, "make one of two mistakes. Either they brag too much, or they are too self-effacing. That's you all over—self-effacing.

"What do you expect me to do?" he continued. "Be some sort of a psychiatrist and pull out the secrets of your personality, analyze them, and then put them together and have me tell you where you fit in our company? It's your job to go over the things you've done and lay them out for me so I can see what you have to offer. If you do that, I'll try to find a place where you fit."

The two went over some of the things Howard had done. In college, he had been a fraternity steward, a job he got when his predecessor was fired after having run the place almost to bankruptcy. In four months Howard wiped out the debt and generated a thousand-dollar surplus. To him it was no big deal. The previous steward had gone wild by serving all the lamb chops the members could eat for lunch and all the roast beef they could eat for dinner. When Howard took over, he served sandwiches at noon and casseroles at night—not a remarkable business strategy in his opinion, but it rescued the fraternity financially. Yet he didn't think someone in business, like Wetherbee, would be very impressed with anything to do with running a college fraternity.

Wetherbee asked Howard why he had been picked for the job over thirty other members. Howard said something about always drawing the long straw and made a small joke about no one else being willing to take the job.

"Stop that kind of talk," Wetherbee said. "You are not talking to some girlfriend you want to impress by being coy. I want to know why you were picked for the job. That will tell me something about you."

Howard answered that he was not altogether sure, except that the members were aware that he had made a nice piece of change from a cigarette business.

"What cigarette business?" Wetherbee had to ask. "I didn't see a thing about that in your résumé."

Howard hadn't thought it was worth telling about, but where he went to college, drugstores ran specials on cigarettes. When there was a sale, he would buy up all he could and lock them in his desk. Then Howard would wait for his fraternity brothers to smoke up their supplies. After all their cigarettes were gone, and they had bummed all they could and were desperate for another cigarette, he would sell them a pack at an outrageous markup. It wasn't a novel idea; other students had tried it. Yet they had all failed, because they fell for the line, "I'll pay you later." Not Howard. His policy had been no money, no cigarettes. Finally, he told Wetherbee he guessed the fraternity elected him steward because he was tightfisted with money.

"Very interesting," said Wetherbee. "Now back to the original story."

"The hard part," Howard said, "was putting up with the abuse from the members. You don't go from lamb chops and roast beef to sandwiches and casseroles without taking a lot of flack. But finally I sold them on it, because I made them see there was no other way to

31

hold the place together, unless they each wanted to put up more money. And that I knew they wouldn't do."

Having uncovered these bits and pieces about Howard, Wetherbee said Howard's next task was to put the pieces together in a way that would appeal to employers. Some parts should be featured as a credential to attract employers, while others should be revealed to show Howard's merit. The order of assembly depended on the occupation Howard wished to pursue.

He chose sales. "Fine," said Wetherbee. "Now, when you see a job listing for a sales position, you can probably get an interview by saying you have had sales experience. But in the interview, expand on that experience by showing the employer that you know something about selling. Investigate selling so that you can talk intelligently about it."

Following Wetherbee's advice, in subsequent interviews Howard guided his remarks along this line:

> Selling cigarettes is really a matter of merchandising—of advertising to create a desire for the product, then of having the merchandise at the right place. In a grocery store, the right place would be on a shelf next to the cashier; in my case, it was my room, which was handy for students. But I felt that my real challenge, the test of my persuasive ability, was in selling my fraternity on the need to . . .

With a more positive approach, Howard's interviews went better. But then he made another mistake. Like other seniors, he followed the pack to such popular employers as IBM, Citibank, and Xerox. As good as Howard had become at interviewing, those corporations had the pick of the crop, and Howard, whose academic record was below average, could not compete.

There were other employers with whom Howard might have had a better chance, but he ignored employers with less glamorous names. Howard finally did take one or two interviews with less prestigious employers at the urging of a counselor, who said, "What have you got to lose? If they offer a job and you don't want it, you can always turn it down."

Howard got an offer, but he didn't appreciate it and did turn it down. He figured he had mastered interviewing and would have an easy time finding just as good a job after graduation when he returned home and called on the employers on Main Street. Turning his nose up at the job turned out to be a big mistake, for job hunting off campus, face to face with American Traditional employers, turned out to be a very different game, as we shall find out next. Traditional employers don't see personal qualities in terms of potential. Their problem, and the problem for job hunters, is that they don't know quite what they want.

Chapter 3

Understanding the American Traditional Employer

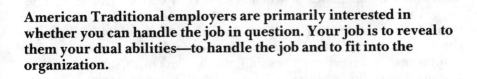

American Traditional employers are primarily interested in whether you can handle the job in question. Your job is to reveal to them your dual abilities—to handle the job and to fit into the organization.

In American Traditional employment, when someone resigns, retires, or dies, the hole in the organization does not start a chain reaction the way it does in the meritocracy, where people are moved up in the game of musical chairs until the vacancy appears as a beginner's job. Traditional employers fill holes at all levels by hiring from the outside or by promoting from within, but if a job is filled the latter way, the ripple effect won't travel much further than the immediate department. You can type employers as traditional when they advertise their openings like this:

Purchasing Agent. Five years' experience in the purchasing of boiler plate and stainless steel. Mechanical engineering degree preferred. Must be cost-conscious.

Or this:

Internal Consultant for strategic planning. Direct and train marketing managers. Partake in group projects in marketing and strategic planning. Develop long- and short-range plans. M.B.A. preferred with a minimum of 3 years' experience in consumer product company. Strong analytical background. Personal attributes should include high energy level. Must be results-oriented, self-starter.

In both listings, phrases such as "cost-conscious," "results-oriented," and "self-starter" are tip-offs to the company's deep concern for personal qualities, but listing them in job specifications is naive. What applicant is going to claim that he isn't results-oriented or a self-starter? The description was probably based on the last person who had the job in an effort to duplicate him if he was good or avoid him if he wasn't. In the case of the latter, watch out! Interviewing such employers will turn out to be an inquisition to try to reveal your weaknesses.

BECOME AWARE OF EMPLOYERS' NEEDS

The interview may seem to go along smoothly while the employer talks about boiler plates or whatever his company's business is. The frustration may not even show up during the first interview. Candidate and employer part with handshakes, each feeling they can come to some kind of an agreement. Later, it begins to dawn on the employer that something is missing, that he isn't quite sure about that person. Why did he leave his last job? Will he be loyal? The job description had said that the right person for the job should be cost-conscious, results-oriented, and a self-starter, and the candidate's application states that he is all of those things. He has supplied all the words the employer wants to see, but somehow seeing them on the application has raised more doubts than belief in the employer's mind. As a result, the employer stalls and stalls. He doesn't have the interviewing skill to find out whether the candidate is really a self-starter or whatever else it is he wants to know.

When interviewers don't seem to be able to get what they want from the interview, you have to sense it and reveal a quality that will satisfy them. You have to reveal a quality in yourself that is universally wanted by employers.

That quality is best demonstrated in an essay in a book by Elbert Hubbard, entitled *A Message to Garcia and Other Essays,* a turn-of-the-century classic that tells the story of Lieutenant Rowan, a hero of the Spanish-American War. During that war, President McKinley needed to send a message to a certain Garcia, but nobody knew where he was. So how on earth could anybody get a message to him? Then someone said, 'There is a fellow by the name of Rowan who will find Garcia for you, if anybody can."

Rowan took the message, and after four days of tramping through the jungle and over the mountains, he found Garcia and delivered the message. Rowan simply did it. He didn't ask, "Was I hired for that?" or "Who is this Garcia?" or "Is there any hurry?" He didn't complain, "Why always me?" Rowan simply took the message and delivered it. Hubbard wove his essay around the virtue of simply getting things done.

"Civilization," Hubbard wrote, "is one long anxious search for just such individuals. Anything such a man asks shall be granted. He is wanted in every city, town, and village—in every office, shop, store, and factory. The world cries out for such; he is needed and needed badly—the man who can carry a message to Garcia."

Shortly after the essay appeared, orders for reprints began to come in: requests at first for fifty, a hundred here and there, a thousand from the American News Company. Then, the New York Central Railroad asked for a hundred thousand copies. During Hubbard's lifetime, which ended when he went down with the *Lusitania* in 1915, forty million copies were in print, including copies for all the workers on the Russian railroads. In Japan, the Mikado ordered copies for all government workers. Hubbard described a quality that knows no boundary or time.

REFERENCES COULD HELP

If you can make employers see you as a Lieutenant Rowan, your job-hunting worries are over. The question is, how do you do it? Ironically, the Rowans of this world do not realize how special they are. Rowan himself couldn't see what all the fuss was about, and one can imagine him applying for a job by reciting a tedious chronology of all the assignments he had in the service. His record was military, but *what* he did doesn't tell his story. *How* he did it, does.

We wouldn't have known Lieutenant Rowan's story if others hadn't told it. The Commanding General of the Army spoke for him, stating that he regarded Rowan's achievement as one of the most hazardous and heroic deeds in military warfare, a creditable and praiseworthy reference that testified to Rowan's merit. References that testify to merit are an important aid in finding employment, but unfortunately *most* references aren't worth much because they don't say anything. You can help this by giving your reference writer some unusual information about yourself, for instance, an example of something you did well.

MAKING YOUR EXPERIENCE COUNT

Another way to interest employers is to tell them about jobs you have held in the past, but you must do this in such a way that employers will see how your experience relates to their needs. Take the case of Eileen Shanahan. To those who knew her, she was much like Rowan—a quiet, resourceful person who got things done. Her last employer, Gould of Gould's Department Store, rated her as one of the three best merchants he had ever employed, but her attempts to merchandise her talents in Texas, where she had recently moved, had fallen flat. If she had followed her instincts and introduced herself to employers as a person who, after raising four children, had taken a job selling lamps in a department store and become the department manager in just two years, that achievement would have stood on its own merit. Unfortunately, taking poor advice on how to sell herself, she minimized her abilities by telling about them in clichés, using such phrases as "results-oriented with strong personal skills and a proven ability to motivate people." She laid it on thick about "increasing profits" until one employer cut her down with, "So what? The store down the street may have increased profits twice as much." What she failed to tell was *how* she had increased profits.

A STORY THAT ILLUSTRATES COMPETENCE

Eileen started at Gould's in a part-time job, selling lighting fixtures and lamps. Inspired by customers' questions, she went to the library and read up on lighting, design, vision, and energy consumption. She visited competitors to see what they had to offer and noticed that they carried certain types of lamps that Gould's did not sell. Lamps and lighting fixtures were not a profitable item for Gould's, even though the store had tied in heavy advertising with promotional sales to increase traffic. The only bright spot, if you will pardon the pun, was Ms. Shanahan. She was asked if she wanted to take over the department to see if she couldn't turn it around.

Her first move was to eliminate price-cutting sales and promotions. Her hunch that they didn't really increase sales proved correct after an analysis of sales data. She shifted the emphasis of advertising to promote the concept of proper lighting. In the late summer, the time students get ready to return to school, her advertisements stressed good lighting for studying. At the store she rigged up a mannequin slouched in a chair to look like a student—textbook in one hand, Coke bottle in the other, and shoes off with a toe sticking through a hole in one of the unmatched socks. Clothes, a football, weight-lifting equipment, and a guitar were scattered about. It was a picture of total disorder, except for a lamp, well positioned to provide good light for studying. The scene was captioned, "At least he won't ruin his eyes." It made a big hit. The store sold four times more lamps that August than in any other month, including the month before Christmas.

The Importance of Revealing the Right Attitude Toward Work

Instead of trying to impress employers with clichés, she should have been telling them about this and other successful promotions she had arranged at Gould's. Fortunately, she met an interviewer who told her frankly that her flamboyant description of herself did not fit her personality, and even if it did, he did not need a high-pressure promoter. The interviewer was curious. How had this prim, ladylike woman succeeded in retailing? She didn't look the type. What did she do at Gould's? When she relaxed, abandoned the hard-sell tactics, and gave him an unembellished account of what she had done, he changed his tune. "I sincerely wish I had a job for you," he said, "but I don't. However, if you promise to tell other interviewers about your experiences just the way you told me, I will introduce you to employers who do have openings. But first, let me tell you what it was about you that impressed me the most. It wasn't the story about the mannequin—that showed me you had good ideas, but ideas are cheap. People that work here are full of ideas, and they are a darned nuisance because they want someone else to carry them out. It was what you said about going to the library to learn about lighting that showed me that you focused your energies on your job instead of taking the attitude of 'What's in it for me?'

"Now, let's see what openings are around," he continued, as he looked through his files. "Through a personal association, a group of us keep each other informed of our needs. Here is a job as a budget analyst with the marketing department of Sheraton Oil. I'll get you an interview."

Ms. Shanahan read the job description and saw that it called for an M.B.A. or the equivalent of two years' experience in finance. She didn't think she could qualify.

"Ah, but you can," the interviewer told her. "You were in merchandising, and you had to budget. You had to balance the cost of goods and sales expenses against sales targets. You told me how you analyzed what sold and what didn't, then determined the mix of products that you would offer for the best return on your investment. What Sheraton wants is someone who has the sense to do what you did. You do, however, need more technical knowledge, and there is time to get it. The interview won't be until next week.

"Go over to the community college. Find out what texts they are using for their course in corporate finance, get copies, and study them. Then during the interview, when you are asked what you know about corporate finance, you will have answers."

The Importance of Showing Confidence

Ms. Shanahan was still a bit skeptical, but the interviewer gave her more good advice and told her about someone else he had interviewed.

"You have to approach job hunting with a certain amount of nerve and self-confidence," he told her. "Eight years ago, I hired a man named Charles Christopher as a surveyor for some site work on a new factory we were going to build. In the interview, when I asked him about experience, he told me that he had helped survey the right-of-way for Interstate Highway 40. I was so impressed that I never pursued the extent of his experience. Do you know what he confessed to me the other day? That 'experience' wasn't work experience. A friend of his was a surveyor, and sometimes he would go out on the job to keep his friend company. To be helpful, Christopher would do some measuring or hold the pole, so technically he had helped in the surveying for Route 40, and he had learned something about surveying—enough to know that it wasn't all that difficult to learn. Obviously, he had absorbed enough knowledge about surveying to get through an interview with me. After I offered him the job, he went to the library, got out books on surveying, and studied them. Then, he got his friend to spend a weekend with him in the field, teaching him surveying. During his first week on the job, his friend checked over his work every evening to be sure he didn't make any mistakes. He has had a successful career with us. Yesterday, at the age of thirty, he was made a vice-president.

"Looking back, I wonder how I happened to hire Christopher," the interviewer went on. "It was his attitude, I think, the same attitude I spot in you, Ms. Shanahan. When you told me what you did at Gould's, you came through to me as a person who directs her efforts toward figuring out what needs to be done, then does it. That's what an employer wants to hear."

If, after reading about Eileen Shanahan, you sense a disadvantage because you have not yet had a responsible job to draw upon to illustrate your competence, don't despair. Remember, you will be hired more because an employer likes you than because of some special experience. And how much you are liked will depend on your attitude. Lieutenant Rowan illustrated that.

SELL YOUR ABILITIES WITH A GOOD ATTITUDE

The average traditional employers don't want to probe your psyche; they just want assurance that you have a good attitude toward work. You want to convey the idea that you are like Lieutenant Rowan. In many ways, it is easier to create a good impression with unskilled interviewers than it is with trained interviewers who can lay you bare with their "Tell me about yourself" questions. Instead of having to tell your life story to create a favorable impression, you may be able to indicate your abilities effectively by making comments or relating anecdotes. Here are some that other candidates worked into an interview, either in response to a question or in telling about an incident:

I got better grades than most people not because I was smarter but because I worked harder.

How do I feel about detail and tedious work? It's like house painting. I like to put on the finishing coat and see the shine. I hate the preparation—the cleaning, the scraping, and the puttying—but the quicker I get at it the better. When the job is finished and I look at the shine, my real satisfaction comes from knowing that I did a good job because I did the tedious preparation well.

I seemed to have more time for myself in college than most of my friends, yet I worked to pay for my tuition, carried a full course load, and always played some sport. People waste so much time procrastinating. I can't stand to have a job hanging over me. I've got to do it.

How do I get along with people? Well, I think. I make it a practice not to get involved in the complaining that goes on at work. I never criticize anyone I work for or with. People seem to respect that.

One summer I worked on the grounds crew at a park. We were a bunch of college kids, and the supervisor was inept. Everybody goofed off. I couldn't do that, so I worked hard and was happy. The others were unhappy. They blamed the supervisor, but they had themselves to blame.

Once, in the Army, I spent a day with a "goldbrick"—that's a guy who has mastered the art of avoiding work. It was the most tiring day I ever spent. Doing things, getting a sense of accomplishment—that's what I find stimulating.

The Let-Me-Tell-You-About-Myself Interview

Undoubtedly you will run into an employer who doesn't ask any questions that give you the leads you need in order to fill in information about yourself. When an interviewer doesn't know enough to ask you about yourself, you can say, "Let me tell you about myself." A candidate for a teaching position told me of an interview where four professors sat across from her in silence. An old-fashioned clock filled the void with loud ticking. Finally, one professor would ask a question. After the candidate answered, each sphinx would look to the other; then they would turn back and stare at their victim. The clock ticked louder. (Of all the stories I hear about interviews, the weirdest seem to come from academic jobs.)

At best, interviewing is difficult, particularly for anyone inexperienced and untrained in the art. But in facing the four sphinxes the candidate is to blame for not rescuing the situation. She could have broken the agonizing silence by supplying the questions as well as the answers: "Let me tell you why I believe I am a good teacher." That opener not only would have given her an opportunity to tell what she could do but a chance to be liked as well. What interviewer wouldn't like to be let off the hook during one of those deadly silences? More important, she could have displayed an infectious enthusiasm for her discipline and for her love of teaching. Enthusiasm counts.

Sometimes the questions are tough; you must be prepared to handle them.

Why was I fired? Burnout! There has been a lot written about it lately. A job becomes too repetitive and you stop doing it well, but you don't realize it. A lot of consultants are working with employers now to get to the root of the problem so they don't lose valuable people. I wish mine had. I really liked working at that place. I paid a consultant on my own to find out what went wrong and what I could do about it. [He was wise to call his counselor a consultant rather than a counselor or a psychologist.]

I was made a manager, and I didn't like it. I would try to put my mind on the budget and personnel matters, but my mind would keep drifting back to some creative idea I wanted to explore back in the advertising department. I want to get back to work I excel in.

At this point, it would be a good idea to review your autobiography to uncover examples of your behavior, thoughts, and observations that reflect your attitudes. Put them down on paper. Boil them down to pithy sentences you can use in an interview. Go over them with friends, preferably friends who are employers and who would be in the best position to know if your statements sound credible. What you say cannot be disingenuous or it will sound disingenuous. You need a sounding board.

Interview First for Jobs You Care About Least

Some of the first interviews you have with traditional employers should be for the jobs you care about least. If your first interview is for a job you desperately want, you may not do well because of your inexperience in interviewing. You may have had interviews on campus, but you will find that traditional employers make interviewing an entirely new experience. You may even run into interviewers who are real screwballs. Stories about them are legion. One candidate became frustrated trying to explain personal qualifications to an employer who spent most of the time on the floor trying to find a lost paper clip. You also hear tales about employers who talk so much the candidates never get a word in edgewise and of other employers who sit there like the four sphinxes. Be prepared to meet them all. And don't jump to conclusions about an organization just because it has a screwball doing its interviewing. Get an offer and then see what the organization is like. Nobody said you have to accept an offer.

Chapter 4

The Job-Hunting Routine and the Routine Job Hunt

Finding the right job can take time. You and your family should be prepared financially and emotionally for the trials and tribulations of job hunting.

"I have looked over your application, but I couldn't tell which job you were applying for. We listed several."

"Any of them. I'm flexible."

"That's fine, but we are not. We have some square holes and some round ones, and you can't be both round and square. Now what are you, round or square, and which job do you want?"

The candidate didn't get any of the jobs. He was neither round nor square, rather more oval. So every day he watched the want ads, checked the employment agencies, and made the rounds of personnel offices looking for an opening for an oval person. At times, being somewhat protean, he would try to display a roundness in an interview, but somehow he would always be found to be oval.

He was in a dilemma. What should he do? Keep hounding the usual sources of job listings and writing letters of application in the hope of finding an oval opening? If his research is good, he will find the most likely employers and the best agencies and media for conducting an efficient and effective hunt for oval openings. That is one approach. Let's see how well it works.

The Case of Howard Carroll
Part 2: Out on the Street—
The Gray Side of Employment

Just before Howard left college, he called on his placement counselor for advice. The meeting had to be brief, because Howard had only twenty minutes left on a parking meter. In the time they had, the counselor quickly distilled his advice to a few points: Don't rely on employment agencies or on newspaper advertisements. Interview first for information. Don't rely on personnel officers except in the meritocracy. "Howard," he emphasized, "you've got to go directly to the person who has the power to hire you."

Howard Carroll had heard all that before. He had also been told not to go to the employment offices of corporations or other institutions to check on their openings. He had been told that if he wanted a job in sales, he should go directly to the sales manager, ostensibly for advice and information, and then, if the job looked good and he hit it off with the sales manager, ask him for a job. That would be all right, he told himself, if I knew the sales manager.

The key to getting a job appeared to be knowing someone, or so Howard felt as time passed and the people who seemed to be getting jobs were those with connections. That didn't make sense. He knew as many people as anyone else, but not people he could ask for a job, a demeaning thing to do as he had found out when he had asked a best friend for one and been turned down because he didn't have the right qualifications. It had been embarrassing for them both. The friendship was never the same. Howard went to no more friends, which was just as foolish. Had he gone to his friend to *explore* job possibilities for someone with his abilities rather than to *ask* for a job, the story might have been different. He should have put his talent on the line, not himself.

He had also been told that organizations depend upon talent, and that it would be he, not the employer, who would be granting the favor by interviewing. That message began to lose its credibility after four employers in a row treated him like a charity case, the last one being an arrogant man who sat behind a mammoth desk from which he glowered down at Howard, who was sitting in a chair that seemed to have had the legs sawed off to two inches from the floor. Job hunting began to make Howard feel like an untouchable.

It's easy to feel like an untouchable when you are looking for a job. In our society we find an identity through work, by being something—an engineer, an educator, a merchant. When you don't do anything, you are nothing. You don't belong anywhere. You are in limbo. In limbo, there are places that say, "Come to us," and you go because it's easier than going where you don't feel wanted. These places may make you feel even more like a nothing, but they offer you the hope of getting out of limbo, so job hunters flock to them. Although the claims of some experts that only 15 percent of the jobs are filled through the sources Howard used may or may not be true, it is certainly true that 85 percent of the job hunters confine their efforts to these sources.

PRIVATE EMPLOYMENT AGENCIES

Private employment agencies were the most humbling. All of them seemed to look alike to Howard. Invariably, they were located on the second floor of some old building, and the second floor was reached in an ancient elevator, built like an iron bird cage, that struggled slowly upward. A dingy hall with a dirty white tile floor and a lone light bulb hanging from a cord led to the door of the employment office. Howard found that when he said he couldn't type they had nothing to offer him. They wanted him to sign a contract, however, just in case something did come up and they could claim a fee for finding him a job.

In all fairness to private employment agencies, it should be reported that there are many good ones, and Howard found a good agency. *He learned about it by asking employers if they could recommend an agency they relied on for good referrals.* The agency staff gave him encouragement and good advice. More important, they made him feel like an important client rather than a pariah. They got him some interviews he could not have gotten on his own, one of which led to a job offer, partially because the agency intervened. The offer came after Howard had been looking for three months, but not before he had followed some leads down discouraging paths.

Howard had gone to Slick Executive Personnel, Inc., an advising and consulting firm for job hunters. There he was treated like a million dollars until the firm realized he didn't have $2000, its rock-bottom fee. Nevertheless, the staff tried to sell him on letting them prepare a "winning résumé," but when he asked to see samples of such résumés they balked, so he balked. Howard wasn't really their type anyway. Their clientele consisted mainly of unemployed executives and professionals who were willing to pay thousands of dollars for a thorough analysis of their talents, so that the firm could help them prepare a résumé and match them with specific employers. This kind of service is worth the fee if it works, but it can be counterproductive if the firm gets its clients to prepare stereotyped résumés that sophisticated employers can recognize immediately and as quickly reject.

PERSONNEL OFFICES

For the most part, Howard called at corporate personnel offices, where he could either get an interview with a personnel officer or at least have the chance to file an application. If these were perfunctory exercises, they at least gave him the feeling that he was doing something.

Because Howard persevered, even on the well-worn path, he finally got a job offer after a long drought. It came as the result of a call he had made at the Gas and Electric Company months before.

He remembered the call. When he entered the building at the main entrance, the receptionist asked him what he wanted—as if she needed to ask. His forlorn look, his awkwardness in a new business suit, and his apprehension told her to send him to the personnel office where professional, executive, and secretarial candidates were interviewed, not the employment office in the annex where blue-collar workers were hired.

In the personnel office, he found the usual formica furniture, the usual Wyeth prints, the usual green carpet, and a typical, coldly attractive receptionist who impassively handed him an application and motioned to a table where he could complete it. As he sat down, he saw a roomful of silent applicants staring blankly ahead like mourners at a wake. The scene made him laugh out loud. The other applicants looked at him as if he were crazy. Ms. Cold, the receptionist, frowned. An attractive woman who was sharing the table with him smiled and whispered to him, "What made you laugh?" When Howard told her, they both laughed.

The woman said she had needed a good laugh. Job hunting was getting to her. Her children were almost ready to go to college, and it was imperative she get a job to help pay for tuition. Everywhere she applied, though, she was classified as "a housewife." Her experience didn't seem to count with employers; nobody would interview her. She had filled out numerous application blanks only to be told that she would be called for an interview if any openings developed. None did for her.

At that point, Ms. Cold called Howard over, took his application, and gave him the same line, but Howard had better luck than the housewife. Figuring that he had probably ruined his chances for a job because of the commotion he had caused, he almost didn't turn in the application at all, but having put considerable thought and effort into it, he decided he might as well leave it.

He had heard that the utility promoted the use of appliances, gas furnaces, lighting fixtures, and other devices that used electricity and gas, so he sent for their public relations releases to learn something about their program. Then he called on an appliance dealer, a heating contractor, and a home extension agent to learn how the utility promoted the use and conservation of energy. Armed with this information, he included with the application a short description of some of the things he had done that related to the sales and consumer relations of the company. Somebody in personnel was impressed enough to send his application and description to the manager of consumer relations. Although they sat unread for a couple of months, when the manager finally got around to looking at them, he was also impressed, called Howard in, was further impressed, and offered him a job!

Howard had to share the good news with someone immediately. He headed for a neighborhood saloon, where he hoped to meet some of his friends and tell them about his luck. No one he knew was there, so he sat down at the bar next to a stranger, put out his hand, and said, "Hi, I'm Howard Carroll. Can I buy you a drink?"

Meet Brunner Wengen, unemployed, bitter, slightly drunk, and feeling very sorry for himself. Before Howard could tell him his good news, Brunner poured out his own sad story.

The Case of Brunner Wengen—
The Dark Side of Job Hunting

The Brunner Wengen story is about a comedown, or more of a crash.

Brunner lost his job after having had a successful career for many years. In trying to find a new one, he made two big mistakes: one was in believing that his talents would be as sought after as they had been when he was a college senior; the other was in not preparing mentally and financially for a protracted job hunt.

Brunner Wengen graduated from a leading university in 1965 with a B.S. in Mechanical Engineering and membership in Tau Beta Pi, a leading engineering honor society. In his senior year, he was wined and dined by companies trying to hire him. He chose a job with Jetco, a major company in the field of combustion and gas dynamics, not because of any great interest in engineering, but because he saw engineering as a route to management.

Jetco was a growth company, a member of the meritocracy, and it promoted from within. A position in management could be in the offing if he did a good job. Most of all, he chose the job with Jetco because the company was in his wife's hometown.

Twelve years marked by babies, diapers, car payments, a home mortgage, and the PTA proved to be just the right catalysts for his ambition. Throwing himself into his career, he moved up rapidly to senior engineer, then project engineer. Finally, thirteen years after he had started working for the company, he was named manager of the JX project, an important competition for a contract to produce a medium-thrust engine for the Navy's Hummingbird Program.

The only other competitor in the JX project was De Tourneau, a company that had never won a major contract. Because Brunner felt Jetco had no real competition, he decided that his company could get away with modifying a current design rather than developing an entirely new one, a decision that would save the company millions of dollars. The contract seemed all but in the bag. Brunner neglected the engineering, leaving it pretty much to subordinates, and concentrated on buttering up the Navy brass who would award the contract.

Brunner loved the job. He had arrived. He had perks—lunch in the executive dining room, a parking place with his name on it, a call on the company plane, and a family membership in the country club. His wife blossomed, becoming a gracious hostess. The manager's life was the life for them. Then the bomb fell. De Tourneau won the contract.

Brunner's severance arrangements were generous—six months at full salary, two months' use of an office and a secretary to give him a base from which to work in finding a job, and no announcement of his "resignation" for that period so he could hunt for a job as an "employed" manager.

His wife took the news marvelously. What a wonderful opportunity to go to Bermuda to get away from the grind! She did feel, though, that they were lucky she wasn't pregnant again. Or were they? A pregnancy, with no employer paying medical insurance, might have scared them and made them batten down the hatches for the coming storm. Instead, they went ahead with plans to send their children to expensive summer camps and kept their membership in the country club, justifying it as an important source of contacts.

Getting fired is a shock, so a trip might have been necessary therapy. But Bermuda for two weeks? They learned to regret it. Two months' use of an office, a secretary, and a telephone also proved to be too little time. Working out of his home was no answer either. "Daddy isn't here right now," didn't fit the executive image he hoped to project. A telephone answering service was a partial solution, until the service was canceled when the bill wasn't paid. Brunner resorted to pay phones, but when he telephoned an important prospect, he suffered the humiliation of having a voice chime in "deposit twenty-five cents please" just as he got his party on the line. After standing outside a phone booth in the rain for three hours, waiting for a return call that never came, Brunner got drunk for the first time. When the six months had elapsed, and he was off the payroll at Jetco, their bank account hemorrhaged.

No one had prepared the Wengens for the reality of job hunting. The expense and the months of hunting—perhaps up to a year or more of frustration and dashed hopes—were not what they had expected. Brunner had thought that finding a new job would be easy. His qualifications were excellent. Remembering articles he had read in *Fortune* and other magazines about the demand for executive talent, and recalling an Executrend Index that measured the demand, he assumed that managers were needed badly. The *Wall Street Journal*'s section, "The Mart," which listed management jobs, was one source he would use. That, he decided, plus résumés sent to management search firms and a few discreet inquiries made among his executive friends at the country club about openings in their organizations, ought to take care of the matter.

His optimism was reinforced by a job offer from De Tourneau, when it heard he was available. With a big new contract, the company was much in need of engineers. De Tourneau offered Brunner an engineering job with no decrease in salary, but it wasn't a management job. It offered no parking place and no private office, just a desk alongside the desks of all the other engineers, many of whom he had supervised at Jetco. Brunner considered the offer something of an insult.

Brunner was ill prepared to analyze his three options: to try for a job at his present level, to take a step down and join De Tourneau, or to gamble on making a step up elsewhere. Of the three options, the most difficult one to accept is the one that requires stepping down a rung or two to get a new footing for resuming the ascent. It may be the wisest move, but pride gets in the way of judgment. The only way to make an assessment of such an offer is to evaluate the employer's situation. De Tourneau had won the contract; now it needed engineers with experience. Brunner had that experience, plus the ability to take on more responsibility should vacancies arise higher up in the company's management ladder. These vacancies seemed sure to open up; the company was on the move. Brunner Wengen made the wrong decision. He turned down the job with De Tourneau.

From there on, his job hunt went from bad to worse. He spent more and more time roaming around the house in a sullen mood. He refused to seek out any information that would help him find a job, least of all a book his wife bought for him. "I'm not gonna read any damn book on job hunting." (Ah, the macho male. He thinks his is the rational sex, but it is more often women who are willing to get advice and analyze their options.)

With no income, the family's finances were in terrible shape. Their car was repossessed, their mortgage payments lagged. His wife threatened divorce if he didn't do something. "Here," she said finally, "is $3000 that I borrowed from my brother. I want you to go to one of those guidance and management organizations that are advertised in the paper to help people who are out of work. They're expensive, so check them out carefully before you sign up with one."

Brunner should have done what his wife suggested and investigated before he spent the money, but he was ripe for the picking. The people in the first firm he went to played on his ego. They told him his qualifications were so good that they could easily find him an excellent job if he used their service. He signed up with them immediately. As it turned out, their service consisted of preparing a résumé for him and providing him with a list of employers "carefully researched as ideal prospects for your unique talents." Brunner was unaware of how little he was getting for his money. At last, he thought, I am on my way.

One day at a lunch counter, Brunner struck up a conversation with a fellow who was also unemployed. Comparing notes, they discovered that they were each using the same consultant, that their carefully researched lists of employers were identical, and that their résumés were twins except for personal data, the names of their former employers, and their job titles. That experience finished Brunner. By the time he met Howard, he was at the very bottom.

Turning to Howard, he said, "Drink to my new job. I am headed for Idaho to clerk in a sporting goods store started by my hippie brother who I always looked down on because he didn't go to college. And drink to my divorce." With that, he got up and wove his way out the door, leaving Howard to pay his bill.

COPING WITH UNEMPLOYMENT

There are lessons to be learned from the experiences of Howard Carroll and Brunner Wengen:

1. If you are being rejected, try not to take it personally.
2. Your chances of being rejected will be great if you look for jobs where everyone else looks. Numerically, the competition reduces your chances, even if you are well qualified and sell yourself well.
3. Expect some employers to be offensive or disagreeable, so you won't be bothered by their attitude.
4. Be assertive. If you are not, consider joining an assertiveness training group, possibly through a community college or a Y.
5. Begin your job hunt by having interviews first for the jobs you are least interested in. It's a good way to practice interviewing, but most of all, it will help you become accustomed to taking the indignities that you are bound to run up against. Your calluses will develop less painfully if the job doesn't really matter to you.
6. Be prepared for a long job hunt. Some of the best-run job campaigns take six months to a year if the candidates are looking for something special.
7. Job hunting is expensive. It takes money for the campaign and living expenses. Job hunting calls for battening down the hatches on all other spending.
8. Read more than one book on job hunting. You can't get too many ideas.
9. Have your spouse and family read these books. They need to know what you are up against to be able to share the burden with you.
10. After your spouse and family have read these books, they will qualify as sounding boards for the strategies and techniques you would like to use. You need sounding boards.
11. Find friends who have gone through successful job hunts. Find out what they did. Ask them to run you through a mock interview. Use them as sounding boards. You need impartial opinions as well as those of your family.
12. If a job hunt begins to get you down, do something physically active, such as playing on a basketball team. You need to have the assurance of belonging to a group. If you can join a musical group or act in a play where you will get applause, do it. You need

applause. You need something that will take you out of yourself. You need an ego-building experience. Job hunting drains you. You must do something that will speed up the tempo of your life.

A BETTER WAY

The tragedy of the Brunner story is that it need not have happened, and Howard didn't have to experience quite so much discouragement in his search. There is help for them both. There is another approach to employment other than the traditional paths pursued by Brunner and Howard. Howard should have used it. He was advised to do so by his college placement counselor. That advice could almost be stated as a principle:

> Most jobs are never listed openly. Go to people who have the power to hire you and seek their advice about getting into the kind of work they do. Interview for information, and if you like what you hear about the work, apply for a job.

Howard tried this, but like most people who try information interviewing, he used the technique as no more than a pretext to get an employment interview and it failed. It didn't even fool the receptionists sufficiently to get him past the front desk and into the office of "the person who has the power to hire." Howard missed the point. The purpose of information interviewing is to find out what an employer needs in order to see if it fits what you want and what you have to offer. *Only when you uncover a need you can fill, and want to fill, should you market your talents.*

Chapter 5
Uncovering a Job: Marketing Yourself

Take the time to uncover hidden needs. Then sell your ability to fill those needs.

"Mr. Munschauer, what's the big idea of filling that job in the Career Center with someone who majored in Russian literature? Didn't you tell us you were looking for candidates with degrees in student personnel—people with some experience as dormitory counselors who could work with the dormitory staff to develop a career awareness program?"

"I apologize, and I hope I haven't put you people in the personnel department in an embarrassing position. A young man who graduated a couple of years ago came to me recently seeking information and advice about the possibility of making a career in placement and career planning. We began to talk about some of the problems I have in getting information to students, and in the course of the conversation, I realized that my problem was one of getting information not just to students in the dormitory but to the entire university community, including the faculty. He had some ideas about how to do it, so I hired him!"

That young man turned out to be one of the best people ever to work in our Career Center. He had the good sense to interview me for information to see if there was a need he could fill, and when he saw that there was, he sold me on his ideas. That's what information interviewing is all about. It all began with a letter he sent to me:

Dear Mr. Munschauer:

I have been looking into placement and career advising as a possible career, although I seem to be approaching the field from a different direction than most people. I have asked for an appointment with you because I want your advice. I graduated from college two years ago, and since that time I have been working in advertising with <u>Network</u>, a weekly newspaper. In college, I was also active on the student newspaper.

What interests me most is the problem of communicating information. For example, when I was a student I used your Career Center extensively and credit it with getting me my job here at <u>Network</u>, yet in talking to my peers while in college I found few of them taking advantage of the information available in the Career Center or even realizing that they needed information. Two years after graduation I still run across classmates floundering in the job market, and they don't know why.

Here is a challenge that strikes me as interesting and important—getting across to students the information that they need to land a worthwhile job. Are there jobs in career planning that might be entitled "information specialist"? If so, are they suitable stepping-stones for moving up in such a career?

These are but a few of the questions I want to ask. Your secretary has given me an appointment for 9 A.M. on Thursday, but I thought it might be helpful for you to know why I want to see you. I am looking forward to our meeting and to getting your advice.

Sincerely yours,
(signature)

When I read the letter of course I knew the writer wanted to employ the well-known technique of information interviewing, so I wondered whether he really wanted information or was just using a pretext to find out about a job. Probably both, but that was all right with me providing it wasn't all pretext. Like most employers I am flattered when asked for advice. But I don't like to waste my time in a conversation that can't go anywhere when I don't have an opening, which I didn't think I had for someone with his background.

Upon his arrival, he opened the interview with questions about the feasibility and wisdom of pursuing a degree in student personnel; then he asked me how I and the other key members of my staff got started in our careers. It's flattering to have someone say, in effect, you are successful and I would like to follow in your footsteps. It warmed me up as it does most people when they get a chance to talk about themselves and their work.

Then we discussed the problem of communicating with students on a campus the size of ours and found that we shared similar concerns. We discussed such things as establishing a career newspaper, publishing a bibliography of career literature, and developing guides to applying to law and other graduate schools. The more we talked, the more career avenues became apparent to him, and the more it became apparent to me that we should create a job for him.

A MARKETING APPROACH

There are paths to careers, and a marketing approach to job hunting calls for finding out what they are. In my field, some enter via professional graduate study; others, as in my own case, are hired because they bring relevant experience from another field. "Once a secretary, always a secretary," so goes the saying. But in our office more than one bright college graduate has started in a clerical position and worked up to a professional assignment. Except for a few scholarly professions where schooling is a must, there is usually more than one path to travel to get where you want to go. Good market research calls for finding the paths and getting some idea of what it is like to travel them.

See what others have done, but remember, the paths they traveled are historical. Yours is in the future and nobody has been there. Anyway, it's the vehicle on the path that does the traveling, and you are the vehicle. A vehicle can cut its own path.

To appreciate yourself as a vehicle, model your marketing approach on computer sales. To invert an old saying, invention can become the mother of need. That is what happened with computers. The computer industry wouldn't be where it is today if its representatives called on engineers, accountants, and administrators just to say here is a computer and here is what it will do. They discussed engineering, accounting, and administrative problems, and when one surfaced that the computer could solve, the sales representatives made their case. They created customers. More important, as representatives looked into the needs of potential customers, they learned more about the potential of computers, and the market grew and grew.

Job hunters have more potential than any computer ever invented, and if they look into employment possibilities in the spirit of marketing, they, too, will discover things to do that will greatly expand their job possibilities.

The analogy is particularly apt for job hunters who must look for a job but don't know quite what they want to do or can do. No computer salesman would ever set forth to call on a customer without a knowledge of the customer's business, and no job hunter should ever seek an information interview without doing homework about the company.

Suppose you get a notion to look into a job with an investment firm. A good indication of your interest in that line of work might be that you read the *Wall Street Journal* regularly and have bought a few shares of stock from time to time. Why not look into the investment business to see if there is something in it for you? Your reading of the newspaper has already given you a start on your preparatory research. Now, you should talk to the broker who sold you stock and read some of the information in his office from investment advisory services. You might even begin to think about working for one of these services. Read more. Get some books on investment research.

MAKING CONTACTS

When you are sufficiently informed to ask some intelligent questions, get an appointment with a market analyst. Your broker can give you some names and possibly help you get an appointment. You might start by talking to someone at a fairly junior level in the hierarchy of an organization to get a yeoman's view of the business. Work your way up to interviews with people at higher levels. If you read a book or an article by an analyst, write to tell the author you like it and to ask for an appointment.

By now you know quite a bit about the brokerage business. More important, you have gotten around. You have established quite a network of contacts whose names you can use to get interviews with the people who "have the power to hire you."

UNCOVERING LEADS

Soon you are able to get an interview with the director of research of a large brokerage house. You must get her talking about her business and herself. How she sees the business. Her investment philosophy (it should be compatible with yours). Discuss your reading and your investigations thus far. (Will she be impressed by the thoroughness of your research?) Then ask for advice. Have some questions ready that relate to her business. If she mentions a statistical approach to investing and you have studied statistics, bring yourself into the picture. If you have spotted a job in her organization that you think you could do, or could learn to do, ask if it is a suitable position in which to start a career. Ask her how she would start if she had to do it over again.

If you handle yourself well, the conversation might work around to discussing employment. If it doesn't come up naturally, it would be more propitious to mention your interest in the work in the letter you write thanking the manager for the interview. If you are interested in employment, there are any number of ways to proceed—a letter, a phone call, a second visit, or a combination of these. You will have to size up the situation to determine your best move. The follow-up is easy; establishing the need and putting yourself in the picture is the important part.

SOME EXAMPLES

My mind keeps going back to Brunner Wengen. With little imagination, and like everyone else in town looking for a job, willy-nilly he called on the most obvious employers, those that are well known and have the biggest buildings. The obvious Gas and Electric Company is where he went next. Had he used a marketing approach there and thought about a possible opening in terms of the company's needs, something might have developed. Brunner's work with jet engines had involved combustion and gas dynamics, a subject of considerable interest to utilities.

Instead, Brunner simply completed an application blank and handed it and his résumé to Ms. Cold, the receptionist. Did his application say anything about his knowledge of combustion and how he saw it relating to generating electricity? Had he redone his résumé to highlight his knowledge of combustion? No, he still used that $3000 résumé prepared by the consultant. It said loud and clear that he was a jet-engine engineer, and of course Ms. Cold, being very efficient, knew her company did not make jet engines. After telling Brunner they would get in touch with him should anything develop, she stuck his application in a file labeled "Untouchables."

At the least, like Howard Carroll, Brunner should have attached a statement summarizing experience that might be of interest to the utility. Better yet, he might have written a letter directly to the engineering department to tell them what he had to offer. Still better would have been for him to go directly to the chief engineer to outline what he knew that might pertain to the utility's needs.

Ironically, the utility had been advertising to no avail for a combustion engineer. The ad had included a job description and specified in detail a list of qualifications applicants had to meet.

How we love to stereotype jobs and people. A marketing approach helps to get around stereotypes, and it doesn't always have to center on an employer's needs, as I found out from a housewife.

The Housewife

Do you remember Lieutenant Rowan, Hubbard's hero? Meet a Lieutenant Rowan, the kind of person every employer dreams of hiring but has a hard time discovering. On every application she listed her occupation as "housewife," stereotyping herself as a person without experience—a familiar story.

With increasing discouragement, she had trudged from employer to employer. She followed the ads. She hounded the employment agencies. She couldn't even be rejected for a job, because she couldn't get an interview. No one had a job listed for a housewife with no "experience." It got to the point where she didn't even care if she got a job; she just wanted to be interviewed. In desperation, she went over a list of acquaintances, people she was sure would give her an interview if she asked for it but who were not such close friends that the friendship would intrude on a business discussion. She picked someone she knew through church activities, the vice-president of a business. She went to him and said, "Please interview me."

"What for?" he asked.

"For no reason other than the experience. I have been looking for a job for months, and none of the job descriptions has matched my qualifications. I would feel a lot better if I could at least have an interview, so please interview me for no reason at all. I manage a household of five people, which means that my receipts and expenditures run into five figures. I have learned to purchase carefully, and by taking advantage of tax allowances and by managing my cash flow to keep all money working in interest accounts, I keep our cost of operation from 10 to 20 percent under the figures published by the Bureau of Labor Statistics for a typical family. I invest the money we save, and right now, I am playing the options market. I keep the books for our church, and I plan and organize the church's biannual campaign for pledges, which means recruiting twenty canvassers, assigning them to territories, and arranging meetings. I prod, push, and cajole the canvassers to get their pledges in on time. I also wrote, designed, and had printed a brochure to show the members of the church how their contributions would be used. I . . ."

She could not get any more words out because the vice-president started to laugh—not to make fun of her but because he was delighted. He had been thinking about adding someone to his staff who could help arrange meetings and conferences when the company brought in its salesmen and distributors for training and planning sessions. It would be an ideal part-time job for her. He asked her if she would be interested.

She sure would. It turned out to be a perfect spot for someone who wanted some money and an outside interest but still wished to save some time for her family.

If the vice-president had listed a job for a "conference planner," you can be sure that the job description wouldn't have mentioned a housewife. In fact, the description would have precluded hiring a housewife, a liberal arts graduate, a teacher, a librarian, or a good many other capable and sensible people who could do the job well if their abilities rather than their titles were considered. It is unfortunate that our credential-happy society has a habit of stereotyping people before we know anything about them.

Rather than damning the system, though, it is better to get around it as the housewife did, with her reverse twist to information interviewing. She started the interview by giving him information about herself without any concern for a job. At the outset, if he had seen her as applying for a job, he would have immediately labeled her as a housewife, and of course he didn't have a job for a housewife. Here are more turn-off labels for job hunters and what the labels signify to employers:

History Ph.D. (for nonteaching jobs). Candidate is overqualified, impractical, and would leave as soon as a job in the field of history came along.

Peace Corps Volunteer. Too idealistic for the practical world. We don't need a do-gooder.

Unemployed. What happened on the last job? Probably fired.

Liberal Arts Graduate. She didn't learn anything useful.

Veteran (especially an infantryman). Probably got to be a bum in the Army. Who wants someone who shoots people?

If you carry a label that is a disadvantage, do what the housewife did. Turn it to an advantage. Involve the employer in your problem, and seek his advice for the solution. Someone with a Ph.D. in history might seek a job in publishing as an alternative to teaching and begin his investigation by sending a letter like this:

Dear Mr. Doubleday:

I have been studying history under Professor Morrison, whose work you have published. Unfortunately, the track I have been on, teaching, has come to a dead end. There are no jobs in it. I have to select a new career. Among the fields I am investigating is publishing, which is not too surprising for one who has spent half his life with his nose in a book and the other half editing and correcting his own work as well as the work of students. In looking into publishing, I have talked to [etc., etc.]. As a result, I have many questions. Professor Morrison suggested I get advice from you. . . .

A CONFUSED JOB HUNTER WITH EXPERIENCE NO ONE WANTS SEEKS ADVICE AND GETS A JOB

Howard Carroll, who had the label of liberal arts graduate, picked up two more labels: veteran and infantryman. After four months on the job with the Gas and Electric Company, he received an offer from the United States Army that he couldn't refuse.

After his tour of duty in the Orient, coming home was a cultural shock not unlike the one immigrants experienced when they saw the Statue of Liberty for the first time. "I'm lost and confused," he said to himself. "I don't think I want my old job back, but I have absolutely no idea what else I want to do or can do."

We could easily change the scenario and have Howard saying, "I am lost. For five long years I have immersed myself in the study of medieval history to the point where I feel like a fourteenth-century Frenchman, and here I am in twentieth-century America with a graduate degree and nonexistent job prospects. I have no idea what to do." He could also have been cast as a liberal arts student whose ambition to become a doctor has just been torpedoed by admissions directors. Or we could have made him an engineer who never had to hunt for a job, having been recruited by a fast-moving, hi-tech company that eventually went broke and left him wondering what happened. Life after an engineering degree is supposed to be secure, and no one is more lost than a person who has worked his heart out in college to earn a place on the security train only to have it derail. Whatever the scenario, it is no fun being confused and having no idea of what to do.

If you don't know what you want to do or can do, you can become confused or you can realize that because you do not have any preconceived notions, your options are open. It's up to you to find out what they are. That is the perfect state of mind to have in beginning a job hunt, and it's the one Howard decided to adopt. It led to a job hunt that turned out to be enjoyable and fruitful even though it had been carried out during a recession in which jobs were supposed to be scarce.

The Case of Howard Carroll
Part 3: Job Hunting Is Brighter the Second
Time Around

Getting called up for military duty after finally landing a decent job had been a hard blow to Howard. Then army life, combat, living in a strange land, and coming home to a culture he no longer felt he knew had left him confused. Why, he wondered, had he been so anxious to get a marketing job when he graduated? He guessed he was just following the pack, because it was the kind of job most of his classmates were after. The members of the class before his had followed a pied piper that led them to banking. However, he wanted a broader view of possible careers, even though he also expected to check out his old job at Gas and Electric to see if he could get it back.

He asked his parents to go over a list of their friends to see what their jobs were. One was a hospital administrator, another built houses, and one was a customs broker. That last kind of job sounded different; he would check it out. While he shied away from asking friends for a job, he didn't mind going to them for information and advice. He went through the Yellow Pages of the telephone book, noting printers, advertising agencies, travel agents, social service organizations, and newspapers that might be worth looking into. But first he went to visit Val Desere, his old boss at Gas and Electric, to see what was going on there. Howard hadn't been too happy in his job there, working with appliance dealers, but if there was an opening in the business development division, where he could work with industry, he thought he would like a crack at it.

While he had been away, his old department had been virtually eliminated, but he did get to see Val, who was now a vice-president of the company. Val couldn't promise Howard anything in industrial development, but he mentioned that the Port Authority was doing some interesting things to encourage the use of the port. A Mrs. Watt was in charge of the department. Howard put her name on the list of people he wanted to see, but there were other organizations he wanted to check out first—places that were not high on his list. He did not know how information interviewing would work out, so he thought he had better try it first at a place where he didn't care if he made a bad impression.

Information interviewing went well. Some of the places that he did not think would be of interest were. He made good contacts. Encouraged, Howard made his way to the Port Authority, where a receptionist wanted to know why he wanted to see Mrs. Watt. She sized him up as another person who was using the line about wanting information as a pretext for getting a job interview.

"What you want," she said, "is the personnel department. Take the elevator to the fifth floor."

"No, I guess I didn't make myself clear," Howard said. Ingenuously, he continued, "I couldn't possibly go through a job interview. I don't know yet what I want to do, so I am not sure of what I have to offer, and I certainly don't know what the department needs. I have been on a foreign assignment with the Army for the past few years, and I need to get reoriented to civilian occupations. I am here for information and advice. If I learn that I have something to contribute, then, and only then, will I apply for a job."

The receptionist thought him strange, but she sympathized with him, although she was reluctant to send him to see Mrs. Watt, the department head. She could be fired if she let a nut like that get past her. "I'll tell you what," she said, "Mrs. Watt is terribly busy, but if you come back tomorrow, I think I can get one of the junior executives to show you around."

Howard was angry. This time, he was not going to sit around in waiting rooms or talk to people who couldn't do anything for him. He wanted to see Mrs. Watt, and right then. If he had learned one thing in the Army, it was that rank counted, and if you didn't have rank you used someone else's. He countered, "It would be helpful to talk to a less-senior executive, but that puts me on the spot. Mr. Val Desere, who is the vice-president of Gas and Electric, was quite specific about my seeing Mrs. Watt, and I think it might be a bit embarrassing all the way around if I didn't at least pay a courtesy call on her." I hope no one checks this out too far, he thought to himself; all Desere had done was mention Mrs. Watt's name. But Howard's ploy stopped the receptionist in her tracks, and she agreed to find out if Mrs. Watt could see him.

As it turned out, Mrs. Watt thought Howard sounded interesting and was willing to talk to him. The meeting went well. Mrs. Watt would have liked to hire him, but the number of positions in her department was rigidly controlled and there were no openings. Howard appreciated her interest and pointed out that he was not ready to apply for a job at the moment anyway. The two agreed to stay in touch, and she offered to be a source of information about other employers in town.

After that, his interviews continued to go well. Some were with friends of the family; then the circle began to spread out to friends of friends. As his shyness disappeared, he found himself calling on executives at a fairly high level without any introduction. Presidents of corporations were just as flattered to be asked for advice as were trainees. "How did you happen to get into merchandising?" or "What made you choose government service?" were the kind of questions that helped to get people talking and evoked informative responses. One observation was reassuring: Howard found that people in comparable positions had started as anything from a secretary or an office boy to an M.B.A. in an elite training program. He came to the conclusion that the person was more important than the job, and the important thing was to get started at any level.

How to Get Employers to Describe What They Do

Sometimes, he found that after employers finished telling him about their own careers, the interview would go dead. He could revive it only if he was prepared to ask intelligent questions, so he made sure he was always prepared. For instance, if he called on an advertising executive, he read up on advertising first. Most frustrating, however, were the employers who were unable to explain what they did in a way that would help Howard see himself in their shoes and understand their needs. One banker said he set policy. When asked for an example, he explained that branch banks were governed by policies, and if a branch banker wanted to deviate from the general policy, he would set a policy for the branch banker. But what policy? He couldn't give a specific example. The interview was useless.

Later, Howard talked to a younger person in the same bank who had been there only a few years and had worked on the kinds of projects a young person like Howard might be expected to tackle if he got into banking. The conversation started along the same frustrating lines, so Howard switched tactics. He asked the banker what he had been doing before being interrupted. Could he tell him something about the papers on his desk? (Howard found this to be a good way to get people talking about their daily work.)

The banker picked up a folder, explaining that it was the file on a company that owed the bank a great deal of money and wanted to borrow still more. The firm had once been a good customer but was becoming slower and slower at repaying debts. Its out-of-date products were selling poorly, but it had potentially good new designs entering production. The folder included a number of reports, including an inventory of the company's assets and a report from a consultant who had assessed the market for the new products. The banker's role in this case was to combine all the data in a report of his own for the loan committee so it could make a decision.

Relating Relevant Experience

Howard remarked that preparing the report reminded him of doing term papers in college, a chore he was good at. Although he was a neophyte in matters of business experience, Howard could imagine himself in this job. The banker agreed that the skills needed were very much the same and encouraged Howard to apply to the bank for employment.

Howard chalked up banking as a career possibility, but he continued to think about other things that might interest him. He liked boats, having been raised in a city with a good harbor, many boat yards, and several boat manufacturers, so he decided to see what the boat industry offered. Not being an engineer or a naval architect, he reasoned that his best bet was marketing; unlike boat design, marketing would not require a technical degree. To learn how boats were marketed, and who did what, he started with a boat yard to get a general idea of the business. Most of all, he wanted to get a line on the people at C and O Yachts, from whom the owner of the yard had received a franchise. The owner told him a C and O representative called on his company at least once a month to work out the next order for yachts, to plan local advertising campaigns, to review and adjust customer complaints, and to audit the yard's finances. Howard also learned that representatives of the larger manufacturers like C and O, who recruited new dealers, were quite interested in local real estate trends, because there was no point in having a dealer too far from a good launching site—or in having a site in a city when a good one nearer a resort might become available.

The more he looked into becoming a representative for C and O, the more he liked the idea. The job involved more than just selling; it included planning, promotion, business strategy, and finance. Up to now, he had learned about the business only from the point of view of boat yards. He wanted to get a view from the manufacturer's side, so he arranged an appointment to see the marketing manager of Piranha Boats, whose products he did not like. No point, he figured, in showing off his naiveté in a place where he didn't want to work. As it turned out, the interview went better than he had thought it would. Piranha suggested that he return to discuss a job if he decided to enter the boat business.

Finally, the big day—time to tackle C and O Yachts. He had learned all he could about the boat business and had decided that it interested him; now, he would try to see the sales manager at C and O about a job. He was stopped cold by the receptionist.

"I know what you want," she said, sizing up Howard as an applicant from his well-scrubbed look, "but how do you 'junior executives' hear we are going to have a training program before we even announce it? Take an application blank," she went on, "fill it out, and leave it with me. If you are one of the people we decide to interview, we will call you. Don't you call us. But I think it's fair to tell you that it could be three months before we do any hiring."

Nuts, Howard thought, but he was glad she had opened her mouth before he opened his. He wanted an interview, and he wanted it then, and from his experience interviewing for information, he knew how to get it.

Quickly he changed his tactics.

"I'm not here for an interview," he said. "I am just out of the service and beginning to look into things, including the boat business. I have some ideas I would like to check out with your manager. I want his advice."

That stopped her. It stopped him, too. Why hadn't it occurred to him before that he was having excellent luck getting employers interested in him by asking them about their business? As each conversation unfolded, he had brought himself into the picture whenever he had something to offer. Howard had been unconsciously marketing himself. He remembered how the fellow at Piranha had kept trying to offer him a job when Howard interviewed him to learn about the boat business. Dumb me, he thought, I was catching fish and throwing them back because it wasn't the way I was supposed to catch them.

The receptionist now had a request that she could not answer, so she excused herself to discuss the matter with the manager. Back she came with a question, which Howard answered with a question, sending her back to the manager. Soon Howard had her bobbing back and forth. When you are fishing and the bobber is bobbing, you know you have a bite, and he sensed he had one now. Sure enough, out came his fish, the manager, who leaned over the rail that divided the waiting room from the inner sanctum and asked Howard what he wanted. Howard told him and was invited in. Howard had done his homework. Having already scouted out the boat business, he was able to ask intelligent, penetrating questions. Impressed by Howard's knowledge and interest, the sales manager began to open up and talk about his work.

He told about the problem of finding suitable locations for boat yards, citing the case of Boston, where waterfront development was attracting people who wanted to keep a yacht in a slip outside of their apartment. Howard drew a parallel with his experience in the infantry, where maps, terrains, people's habits, traffic lanes, and supply lines all determined strategy. They drew another parallel: the problem of expediting orders in business with that of getting supply lines going in the Army—a task that took more ingenuity in a combat area than it did in any business.

If Howard had approached the boat dealer as an infantry officer, both the sales manager and Howard would have wondered what leading soldiers in combat had to do with the boat business, but by drawing parallels, each discovered that it took the same qualities to be a good army officer as it did to be a good businessman. It occurred to Howard that many of these same qualities had applied to his being steward at his fraternity and to his success as a student.

Their conversation warmed as they found more in common. Suddenly the sales manager said, "Say, I would like to hire you. We don't have a suitable job at the moment, but I could make a place for you in the mailroom until something opens up. That would make a great learning spot. You would see the orders come in, read customer inquiries, and see problems reflected in complaints."

Howard had a job offer, with a promise of a more suitable job soon. He had discovered the potential of information interviewing. He continued to seek advice and information, while bringing into the conversation his own experiences as they related to employers' needs. When he was interested in a job (it was unusual for one to be offered on the spot), he followed up the conversation with a letter of thanks, a résumé tailored to the employer's needs, and a request that the employer let him know if there was any chance of a suitable job opening up.

PRINCIPLES OF INFORMATION INTERVIEWING

Step by step, let's review the case of Howard Carroll to establish principles for information interviewing.

First and foremost, *the purpose of information interviewing is to discover where you fit—where you can make a contribution and find satisfaction.* Looking back, Howard realized that when he had looked for a job at the time of graduation, he had followed his peers into the occupation that was most attractive at the time. Following the pied piper isn't the way to pursue a career.

Second, *to get a job offer, you must impress employers favorably.* Howard learned how to do that by putting employers' interests first in the exploratory phase of job hunting. If I were an employer, and you wanted to make an impression on me, what should you do? Immediately tell me all about yourself, or get me to talk about myself? Or turn this around. Who flatters you most—the person who gives you advice, or the one who asks for advice?

I don't think the manager at C and O had ever had anyone come to see him who cared a hoot about what he did. He became interested in Howard not because of any clever résumé or exceptional interview skills but because Howard was interested in him and his problems.

The third point may be the most important. *Interviewing is something of a poker game. Through information interviewing, you can get an employer to lay down his cards before you show yours.* When the manager at C and O mentioned market research in relation to the strategy of locating dealers, Howard laid down a card that fitted by telling about a related experience. If, during an information interview, Howard wasn't able to make a match, he kept his mouth shut, and no harm was done. By asking questions, he didn't have to lay down a card in ignorance that might have thrown the manager off the game.

I see candidates barging into interviews, showing employers their résumés, and stating their job objective before they understand the employers' objectives and needs, and it is *their* needs and *their* objectives that create the jobs.

The fourth point is related to the first. *Look at work to learn more about yourself and to understand the employer, and if there is a fit, steer the interview so that the fit becomes obvious to the employer.* The essence of a job is what needs to be done. Interviewing at times seems to focus on personality and traits. Important as your traits are, remember that the ones that matter are those that relate to the job. They should become as clear as possible to employers through a discussion of *their* situations, *their* work, and *their* problems.

Fifth, *the search for a job and a career is a game.* When employers are doing the interviewing, you play it on their terms. It becomes something of an inquisition, and an inquisition is a defensive exercise. You don't get down to the essence of the work. However, if you do information interviewing, you play the game on *your* terms. While you are trying to draw employers out by addressing yourself to their needs, what you are really doing is finding work that you can relate to your basic needs, talents, and wants. Information interviewing is your best way to gain a vicarious experience.

Sixth and last, *information interviewing, unlike the inquisition, is fun.* The vicarious experience you gain will prove useful time and again in whatever career you choose.

WHY INFORMATION INTERVIEWING WORKS FOR SOME AND NOT FOR OTHERS

Information interviewing isn't all that new. Those of us who hunted for a job long before the technique became formalized did information interviewing of a sort. We talked to people to find out what employers were like. If we had an idea we might like advertising, the most natural thing was to talk to an advertising executive for an insider's view of the industry. If we didn't know somebody in the business we would sound out friends who might be able to open a door for us. One door led to another. Not uncommonly, people were not only generous with their time but would introduce us to others who could be of help. Sometimes they would tip us off to who was hiring. People are not all that different today, although conditions have changed.

During the thirty or so years of economic growth following World War II, there was a shortage of talent, so employers pursued good candidates. As a result, job seekers did not need extensive investigation and contacts in order to find work. But the current situation is historically more typical, with candidates actively pursuing employers. In the thirty boom years, however, the old system of investigation and contacts was forgotten while at the same time a more complex economy emerged, making it more difficult to obtain information and develop contacts.

Today we have rediscovered these old techniques, given them the titles "networking" and "information interviewing," and refined the techniques to deal with the complexities of employment inherent in a modern industrial society. As so often happens, however, good ideas become clichés. Instead of information interviewing being used for gathering knowledge that will help in figuring out the employment maze, it has been used to open an easy path through it. In a way, education has also become a cliché—something that is supposed to provide a career instead of preparing you to develop your own.

When I see education and information interviewing being used improperly—take all the right courses and use the right job strategies and a career will pop open—I think of something I have heard from more than one self-made millionaire. According to them, if you concentrate your efforts on trying to make money, you probably won't. On the other hand, they say that if you become obsessed with an idea such as starting a publishing house or creating a company to make a better mousetrap, and you pursue it despite risks, then you are on the right track.

Howard Carroll succeeded because he didn't set out to use information interviewing as a good way to get a job. He set out to find out what he could do and should do for a living. It's that simple. He didn't think the technique would get him a job; he thought what he found out would. Without Howard's spirit of making his job hunt an adventure in discovery, information interviewing would have been no more than pounding the pavement and knocking on doors.

It should also be noted that Howard didn't call on huge organizations such as General Motors or Bankers Trust. Companies such as these have recruiting booklets that describe hiring practices and job opportunities, so why seek an information interview? Since they spell out their needs, he could figure out whether or not he wanted to apply for a job.

Information interviewing best fits situations where job information and hiring practices are not spelled out, mostly with American Traditional employers where, not incidentally, employment prospects are most fertile. For example, in 1985, according to *Business Week* (May 27, 1985), most new jobs were created by such companies as Artistic Greetings, in the greeting card business; Styker, making battery-powered surgical instruments; Comair, a commuter airline; Dreyer's Grand Ice Cream, purveying premium ice cream; and Ero Industries, making sleeping bags.

Candidates who do call on smaller organizations say that getting interviews is relatively easy. Yet too many of these interviews never seem to go anywhere. As one woman said, "I learned all kinds of things that interested me and I met many employers for whom I would like to have worked, but nothing ever came of it. I do follow up with a letter of thanks and express an interest should anything open up, but that is the end of it." She did not, as it turned out, do as Howard did. He continually brought himself into the conversation by mentioning things he had done that demonstrated a talent of potential interest to an employer. The woman in question wrote very well and ran across several jobs in which writing was important, yet she didn't mention anything about her writing.

Before an information interview you should outline the points you want to cover. Howard outlined his questions like this:

1. How did you get started in your career and what career path did you follow as you moved up to your present job?

2. In the future, what career paths do you see people following as they move ahead?
3. What would a log of your typical day include?
4. Can you describe some typical challenges you face and how you deal with them?
5. Your job is what I would call a "think" job calling for ingenuity and imagination. Is that accurate? If the response to the question is yes, I will cite examples of the way I outline problems, then suggest possible solutions. I can draw on my college experience in preparing for essay examinations or the way I analyzed the financial losses suffered by our fraternity dining room and the possible solutions I outlined. (Howard had read about the occupation and could anticipate that these and other qualifications might be appropriate to bring into the discussion.)
6. When you hire, do you require or prefer graduate training? What are your thoughts on graduate school or continuing education? If graduate study is preferred, ask why. Is it a matter of prestige or getting contacts? If I could get a job without graduate study, what would I miss by way of knowledge? Could I learn on the job?

Preparation is what makes any interview a success. Anybody who would call on Artistic Greetings without knowing something about its products and who has not called on retailers to learn about the business from their point of view deserves to be shot down.

None of this comes easy. Remember, in the beginning Howard cut his teeth interviewing employers who were not of great interest to him. At the outset, to call on preferred employers before you know what you are doing may just discourage you.

There is no getting around it—information interviewing is easier for people who have had some work experience. Howard had no luck with it when he graduated from college. Admittedly, his efforts were perfunctory, but even so, without time in the military to learn more about himself, he would have had trouble bringing out experiences that demonstrated his analytical powers and persuasive abilities, to name two of his talents. Just as important, he spotted things in some jobs that he knew he wouldn't do well.

Working while job hunting—selling door to door, part-time work as a typist, volunteer work, bagging groceries, or any kind of activity—is a good complement to job hunting. Any experience helps in learning. Get out and talk to people. Find out what is going on. Make contacts. Don't try to find the perfect job. You can learn just as much from a poor job as you can from a good one, possibly more. Then, like Howard, you will know more of what you offer and what you want the second time around.

Chapter 6

Communicating Your Message Through Letters and Résumés

Develop letters and résumés that tell employers what you can do for them. You should speak to their needs, not your own.

"I am sorry, Father O'Mega, I can't let you in."

"But, St. Peter, I did everything I was supposed to. I changed the mass from Latin to English. I had the communicants hold their hands the new way when they took communion. Everyone, so far as I knew, genuflected properly, and even Mrs. O'Reilley's Protestant husband stood when I read the gospel. I can't think of a thing I did that was wrong."

"The message, Father O'Mega, what about the message?"

"The message? What message?"

"The message of the Lord, Father. Don't you remember? The Ten Commandments? The Beatitudes? The Golden Rule? It's the *message* that gets people in here, not the ritual. The ritual was supposed to help deliver the message, but you made the ritual the message and the meaning got lost."

Meanwhile, back on earth—

In Tucumcari, New Mexico, and all over the United States, job hunters are at their typewriters and computers pushing words around to make their résumés look like the ones they have seen in books. Whether to use elite or pica, that is the question. Does the résumé have enough action verbs? Should it be printed?

In Peoria, Illinois, and elsewhere employers are scanning résumés. Some are beautiful to look at, a few are even printed commercially on expensive paper. But the résumés are laid aside. Employers are reading them with one thought in mind: What can the candidates do for us? The message they are looking for isn't there.

WHY USE A RÉSUMÉ?

The purpose of a résumé is to convey a message, a purpose easily forgotten in the ritual of preparing it. At every turn, you will get conflicting advice about how to conduct the ritual:

You must have a résumé to get a job.

The purpose of a résumé is to get an interview.

Every résumé must have a job objective.

A résumé should never, ever be longer than one page.

On a résumé, list experience chronologically.

On the other hand, others advise:

Don't use a résumé if you are looking for an executive position or merely seeking information.

Résumés typecast you and narrow your options.

Interview for information first, determine what an employer wants, and then decide whether offering a résumé will suit your purposes.

Two or more pages present no problem if your résumé follows a logical, easy-to-read outline.

List your experience by function, not chronologically.

The more opinions you get, the more confused you become, but you finally work up something. You send it out. You get little or no response. You change your résumé from one page to two pages—or from two pages to one. The results are no better. Somebody says to try pink paper, *that* will get attention. You decide you should have used blue. You fiddle and fiddle with your résumé, trying to find the magic formula that will get you what you want. You are caught up in the ritual, forgetting that the purpose of a résumé is to send a message.

It is hard not to be distracted from the message. You concentrate on developing a format, forgetting the message, instead of concentrating on the message and *then* working on a format that will convey it best. But what is your message? To find the answer, use your imagination to step out of yourself and become an employer. Think about what the employer is trying to accomplish and the talent required to get it done. Now, from your imaginary employer's chair, look back at yourself and ponder the answer. If you can't come up with one, you will have difficulty writing a résumé that will say to the employer, "I have something to offer you."

Résumés are not tickets to a job. They are just one of several ways to court employers. And, as in any courtship, sometimes it's just as well not to put everything in print when the other party might draw the wrong conclusion. Take the case of Cheryl Fender, an alto who learned that the Springfield Opera Company was auditioning for an alto to sing *Carmen*. Cheryl was well qualified, and her voice teacher was well known as a coach of only the most gifted singers. On the other hand, her résumé, which was incomplete, with gaps in her history, showed extensive experience as a secretary. Wisely, she did not send the résumé, because it might have established her as a secretary who wanted to sing, rather than as a singer who had supported herself by being a secretary. Instead, she asked herself, What is important to a director? Voice, of course, so she outlined her training in a letter. But dramatic ability also mattered, so she included pictures of herself on stage in roles that beautifully illustrated her dramatic ability. She got an audition. Cheryl followed a good marketing rule: Don't confuse customers by flaunting things that don't speak to their needs.

GIVING YOUR MESSAGE

While the language of employment for you is "I want" and for employers it is "I need," you can create résumés and letters in your language that will be read by employers in theirs. I don't mean statements such as, "I have analyzed my qualifications and feel confident that they fit your needs." If you were one of the thousands of employers who read this kind of thing, wouldn't you ask, what qualifications and what needs? If the answer isn't clear—and it rarely is—there won't be a message.

It isn't all that difficult to create one that is effective. Think of letters as offering the most creative method to communicate with employers. Even if you are going to be approaching them in person, go through the exercise of writing letters. Otherwise, like most people, you can get caught up in the résumé ritual and neglect to develop the prose that can be more effective in telling your story. People sweat over résumés, then dash off letters without much thought. Perfect résumés arriving in the mail won't even be read if the cover letters don't impress and engage employers.

I recall being asked to review an applicant's proposed application letter for a job on the staff of a yachting magazine. The letter was beautifully written, but it left the impression of being all "I": "I want to write so very much, and I am sure I can learn if you give me a chance . . . I got straight A's in English . . . I love boats . . . I am a sailor . . . I was captain of the sailing team in college. . . ."

What do you say to a person who has written a letter like that? He had obviously spent hours composing it. In its appearance and use of language, it met the highest standards. I could not squelch the young man's hopes, so I had him read *Book Publishing*,[2] a pamphlet Daniel Melcher wrote when he was president of R. R. Bowker Company. Although the pamphlet is concerned only with book publishing, I thought its message would be useful for someone interested in magazines as well.

Let me paraphrase a portion of Melcher's pamphlet:

I like publishing and you might like it too. It is only fair to warn you, however, that publishing attracts a great many more people than the industry can possibly absorb. Sometimes it seems as though half of the English majors in the country besiege publishing offices for jobs each year. While we hope that you will have something to offer us, you might as well face it. Publishers are experts in the art of the gentle brush-off.

The interviewer hopes that you have what he needs, but it turns out that you have never looked into any of the industry's trade journals nor read any books about the industry. You haven't even acquainted yourself with the work of your university press. You tell the interviewer that you are willing to start anywhere, but it develops that a file clerk's job would not interest you, you do not want to type, you don't think you can sell, and you know nothing about printing.

The fact is, all you have thought about is what you want, but it is his needs that create jobs, and you must address yourself to needs.

Your problem, therefore, is to learn as much as possible about the industry before you go looking for a job. Only in this way will you be able to put yourself in the publisher's place and talk to him about his needs rather than about your wants.

After reading Melcher's advice, the fellow said he got the point, thanked me, and left, returning about three weeks later to show me his revised letter. It began in much the same way as his earlier effort—with "I's": "I majored in English . . . I have done considerable sailing . . ."; but after a few short sentences, he suddenly changed his tack. A new three-sentence paragraph began like this: "With my interests, naturally I want to work for you. But more to the point is not what I need but what you need." He followed this with three words that many women refuse to use and that men almost never think to use: "I can type." Right away, he showed that he knew he must be useful.

So much for the easy part of the letter. Next came the difficult part. Although he had had no experience, and had never submitted an article to a magazine or even written for a student newspaper, he still had to come up with something that would interest the editor. He found the solution. The letter continued in this manner:

> . . . In looking into the field of journalism, I visited the editor of
> our alumni magazine, and I talked to magazine space salesmen
> and to executives responsible for placing ads in magazines. I also
> visited a printer who has contracts with magazines. In addition, I
> have been reading trade journals and several books on the
> industry. As I looked into publishing, it occurred to me that of all
> the things I have done, the one I could most closely relate to the
> field was, strangely enough, an experience I had as a baby-sitter.

Immediately, he had the editor's full attention. How could baby-sitting fit in with publishing? During the summer of his junior year in college he had taken a job as a sailing instructor, tutor, and companion for the children of a wealthy family that summered on the coast of Maine. The parents often went away for a week or more at a time, leaving a governess in charge, with a cook, chauffeur, mail, and gardener to do the chores and the student to keep the children busy. While the parents were on a cruise, the governess suffered a stroke, sending the cook into a tizzy, the maid into tears, and the chauffeur and gardener to the local bar. Only the student could cope, and he took charge and managed the estate for the rest of the summer.

In his letter of application he described the crisis, and subsequent problems he had faced, and told how he had met them. Then he related those experiences to the problems that he had learned editors, advertisers, printers, and others encounter in the publishing industry. Reading his letter, you could picture the student working for a publisher. There would be no slipups with the printers. Advertisers and authors would be handled with tact, yet he would get them to turn in their copy on time. He came through as someone with ingenuity, energy, and reliability; and the letter itself testified to his writing ability.

Did he get the job? Yes, and no. He got an offer, but because of the publisher's urgent needs the job had to be filled immediately, and he could not accept it. He was teaching school at the time and felt that in fairness to his pupils he should finish the school year. However, a while later, the letter surfaced again when a group of editors at a meeting chatted during lunch. The subject of good editorial help came up. It followed the usual theme, "They don't make 'em like they used to." The editor of another sailing magazine complained that he had been looking for an assistant, but despite hundreds of applicants had found none suitable. At this point, the editor of the yachting magazine described the young man's letter and agreed to share it. The upshot was, again, a job offer. This time the timing was right, and the young man took the job. There is nothing quite like the staying power of a well-written letter. It is remembered.

Later, I complimented the young man, telling him I had never read a better letter. "It was easy," he said. "The first letter was the tough one. I didn't have anything to say other than 'I have a good record. Please give me a chance,' but I knew everyone else was saying the same thing, so I would have to say it better. I struggled with every word, trying to make an ordinary message extraordinary, but even elegant words can't make something out of fluff. I didn't know anything about publishing, so I didn't have anything to say to publishers; nor could I be really convincing without knowing enough about the work to decide whether I wanted that kind of job or not. But publishing sounded exciting, so I thought I would give it a fling."

The Importance of Knowing What the Job Is All About

"When I looked into the field in depth," the young man continued, "I became confident that I had something to offer. Thanks to a few good high school teachers and college professors, I knew where to place a comma and a colon, so I had a technical skill to offer publishers. And I knew sailing. But the big need I saw was one I discovered when I was teaching school and again when I was an assistant manager at a McDonald's—a need for people who can get things done. Such a quality is hard to describe without an analogy. I could have alluded to any number of jobs I had held, but I chose the baby-sitting job because I thought it would be different and would introduce an element of surprise. Apparently, the analogy worked. I got a job. More important, I wanted it. If I had received a job offer after sending the first letter, before I had really investigated publishing, I would have taken the job with an attitude of 'teach me.' That's a passive role, one of an observer, and observers tend to be critical. The chances are fifty-fifty that I would not have known how or where to contribute and would have quit after a while. Instead of offering my employer solutions to his problems, I would have become one of his problems."

I asked the young man if he had used any other supporting documents, such as a résumé, to help him get the job. "I had a résumé," he replied, "but I held it back, because my task was to transfer the qualities I had demonstrated as a baby-sitter to the needs of a publisher, and I couldn't seem to do that in a résumé. A résumé is a good way to outline facts, but I had to use prose to develop the analogy.

"I did think about including a writing sample, but when I studied the magazine I realized that most of the articles were written by contributors rather than the staff. Their job was to select and edit articles. If I presented myself as a writer, I wouldn't have received an offer; the magazine didn't hire authors. When a friend of mine saw an advertisement for an editing job, he made a list of the required qualifications, then presented his case point by point, right on target. Then the dope attached his résumé that said loud and clear, 'I want to be a writer.' He should have either skipped the résumé or prepared a new one."

Are these examples intended to be good arguments for not using résumés? No. They simply emphasize that it is important to determine the best way to get a message across. There are times when there is no substitute for a résumé. When employers advertise and list the qualifications they seek, there is no better way to respond than to send a résumé outlining qualifications.

LETTERS OF APPLICATION

Sometimes, however, it is hard to figure out how to make the letter of application you send with your résumé more effective than those of the hundreds of people who are responding to the ad. Imagine being on the receiving end of applications at General Motors or Exxon, organizations that list jobs in Peterson's annual *Engineering, Science, and Computer Jobs*[5] and *Business and Management Jobs*[24] and in the *CPC Annual.*[3]

To find out about the effectiveness of letters and résumés, I visited corporations and asked employment managers for their comments. "Here," said one employment manager, as he picked up an eighteen-inch stack of letters and handed it to me. "This is my morning's mail. Read these letters and you'll have your answer."

"I can't," I protested. "I have only two hours, and there's a day's reading here."

"Yes, you can," he replied. "Unfortunately, you'll get through the pack in a half hour, because a glance will tell you that most are not worth reading."

It was hard to believe that the letters could be that bad, but he was right. The typical letter was an insult. Among the letters that I did not finish reading was one on onionskin paper, in very light type—it must have been the fifth carbon in the typewriter. It began:

Dear Sir:

I am writing to the top companies in each industry and yours is certainly that. I want to turn my outstanding qualities of leadership and my can-do abilities to . . .

Enough of that. Also, the applicant hadn't even bothered to type in the employment manager's name, which he could easily have found in the *CPC Annual* or in Peterson's Job Guides.

The next letter was written in pencil on notepaper. There may have been an Einstein behind that one, but I can't imagine anyone taking the time to find it out. Many other letters were smudged and messy. Some applicants tried to attract attention with stunts, such as putting cute cartoons on their letters. One piece of mail contained a walnut and a note that read, "Every business has a tough nut to crack. If you have a tough nut to crack and need someone to do it, crack this nut." Inside the nut, all wadded up, was a résumé. Cute tricks and cleverness don't work at the General Mammoth Corporation.

At the same time, the good letters stood out like gold. Five letters, only five letters in that pile of hundreds, were worth reading. They had this in common:

They looked like business letters. Their paragraphing, their neatness, and their crisp white 8½" x 11" stationery attracted attention like good-looking clothing and good grooming.

They were succinct.

There were no misspellings or grammatical errors.

As I read them, I heard a voice—the voice of a fusty old high school English teacher—commanding out of the past:

If you can't spell a word, look it up in a dictionary.

Use a typewriter. Pen and ink are for love letters.

Clean your typewriter. Avoid fuzzy type. You wouldn't interview in a dirty shirt, so don't send a dirty résumé or letter.

For format, use a secretarial manual. If you don't have one, get one from the library. What do you think libraries are for?

How that English teacher would have loved the following advice from Malcolm Forbes, the editor-in-chief of *Forbes* magazine:

> Edit ruthlessly. Somebody ~~has~~ said that words are ~~a lot~~ like inflated money—the more ~~of them that~~ you use, the less each one ~~of them~~ is worth. ~~Right on.~~ Go through your entire letter ~~just~~ as many times as it takes. ~~Search out and~~ Annihilate all unnecessary words, ~~and~~ sentences—even ~~entire~~ paragraphs.[4]

The following letter is typical of those I saw that day. Give it the Forbes treatment, and see what you can do with it. You may need a scissors as well as a pencil.

Dear Mr. Employer,

I am writing to you because I am going to be looking for employment after I graduate which will be from Michigan where I studied Chemical Engineering and I will be getting a Bachelor of Science degree in June. The field in which I am interested and hope to pursue is process design and that is why I am writing your company to see if you have openings like that. I think I have excellent qualifications and you will find them described in the resume which I have attached to this letter.

The five letters that stood out favorably were characterized by their simplicity. Here is a letter, fictitious of course, but enough like the letter I remember to give you an idea of the ones that created a favorable impression:

February 1, 1986

Mr. Paul Boynton
Manager of Employment
The United States Oil Company
1 Chicago Plaza
Chicago, Illinois 60607

Dear Mr. Boynton:

This June I will receive a Bachelor of Science in Chemical Engineering from the University of Michigan, and I hope to work in process design or instrumentation. I was glad to see your description in Peterson's <u>Engineering, Science, and Computer Jobs 1986</u>,[5] soliciting applicants with my interests. I am enclosing a résumé to help you evaluate my qualifications.

While I find all aspects of refining interesting, my special interest in process design and instrumentation developed while working as a laboratory assistant for Professor Juliard Smith, who teaches process design. I wrote my senior thesis under him on the subject of instrumentation, and part of what I wrote will be used in a textbook he is writing and editing.

Would it be possible to have an interview with you in Chicago during the week of March 1? To be even more specific, could it be arranged for 10 A.M. on Tuesday, March 3? I am going to be in Chicago that week, and this time and date would be best for me, but of course I would work out another time more convenient for you. In any event, I will call your office the week before to determine whether an interview can be worked out.

Sincerely yours,

Charles C. Thompson
1 Riverview Lane
Ann Arbor, Michigan 48106

Thompson's effective letter, and three of the four others, followed a similar pattern:

(1) The first paragraph stated who the writer was and what he wanted;

(2) The second paragraph, sometimes the third, and in one case a fourth paragraph, indicated why the writer wrote to the employer and mentioned areas of mutual interest, special talents that might be of interest to employers, or other factors relating to his qualifications that could be better described in a letter than in a résumé; and

(3) A final paragraph suggested a course of action.

The fifth letter covered the same points in a different order. I remember it because it complemented a good but not outstanding résumé. In that résumé, a perceptive employer might see a person he would like, someone who is energetic and personable. Yet it didn't quite hang together because the work history and activities didn't seem to support what the writer wanted to do. But look at the letter that "made" the résumé:

Mr. Paul Boynton, Manager of Employment
The United States Oil Company
1 Chicago Plaza
Chicago, Illinois 60607

March 10, 1986

Dear Mr. Boynton:

This June, following my graduation from the University of Puget Sound, I want to pursue a career in sales. Between April 10 and 23, I plan to call on leading companies whose products I would like to sell. The purpose of this letter is to determine whether you would like to have me include you in my itinerary.

Let me tell you why I believe I can sell. It seems to me that I am always selling. As a camp counselor, I persuaded the director to buy a fleet of small sailboats so I could start a sailing program. When our college housing co-op needed painting, I persuaded the members to give up a vacation to do the job. In thinking about how I enjoyed selling these and other projects, I decided to look into a sales career. I persuaded several sales representatives to let me spend a day or more traveling with them to see what it was like.

While with them I realized something more about myself that further convinced me I belong in sales. The best sales representatives were well organized, had high energy levels, and used their time efficiently, qualities I feel I have also. As evidence, I have enclosed a résumé that outlines my accomplishments in college and during vacations.

I hope to hear from you, as United States Oil is in the top group of employers on my list.

Sincerely,
Lance Zarote
Encl: Résumé

81

Hard Work and Professional Typing Make a Good Letter

While only the five letters were effective, the rest of those who wrote could have done as well. The point is they didn't. Most people won't. Therein lies your opportunity, because, like Thompson and Zarote, you can write letters that set you apart. You don't have to create a literary masterpiece; just don't hastily knock off a letter with thoughts that wander all over the page. Write it and rewrite it, following Forbes's advice. Unless you are an exceptional typist, you are not good enough to type it yourself. Hire a professional. If you use a word processor, be sure the print is letter quality. Also, get an English teacher or someone in the word business to check your spelling, punctuation, and grammar. But be sure it is your letter. Somehow, a ghost-written letter always has a phony ring to it.

Don't Delegate the Job of Letter Writing

More important than style, however, is the thought process used in preparing letters and résumés. Don't shortchange yourself by delegating your thinking to someone else. When you write to employers, think about their needs; then think about yourself and what you offer, and relate this to what you would like to do. Putting your thoughts on paper—thoughtfully—will make you sort out your ideas and interrelate them. When you see them on paper they will talk back to you, at times to suggest better ideas, at other times to tell you that you are off the mark. To organize your ideas, create an outline. In other words, prepare a résumé even if you decide not to use it. *The value of a résumé is frequently more in its preparation than in its use.*

RÉSUMÉ PREPARATION

When you do give an employer your résumé, make it a testimony to your ability to organize your thoughts. Remember, too, it must look sufficiently attractive to get an employer to read it. Unfortunately, most of the résumés I saw on employers' desks were just as unattractive as the letters; they had sloppy, crowded margins, were poorly organized, and were badly reproduced. At least 30 percent of the résumés had been put aside with hardly a glance because their physical appearance was awful. The rest got a twenty-second scan to see if they were worth studying.

LANCE ZAROTE

Campus Address
101 Morril Hall
University of Puget Sound
Tacoma, Washington 95840
(206) 602-6206

Permanent Address
25 The Byway
Provincetown, Massachusetts
05840
(617) 206-6026

GOAL: A SALES CAREER

EDUCATION: UNIVERSITY OF PUGET SOUND
                                    Bachelor of Arts 1986
               Philosophy Major
               Business-related Courses
               Statistics   Introduction to Computers
               Economics   Calculus
               Accounting   English

EMPLOYMENT: UNIVERSITY OF PUGET SOUND (Work-Study
               Program)
               Dining Hall supervisor   1985–86
               Kitchen helper   1982–84

               OTHER WORK while in college
               Ma and Pa Motel, Tacoma—night clerk   1985
               Joe's Bar and Grill—weekend waiter & bartender
                                              1984–86
               Baby-sitting, gardening, house cleaning   1981–86
               WATCHEE OUTEY SUMMER CAMP, Nome, Alaska
               Sailing coach and waterfront director   1985
               Counselor   1981–84

ACTIVITIES: CAMPUS
               Chair, Campus Chest Drive
               Intramural hockey, tennis, and volleyball
               LIVING UNIT
               House Manager, $25,000 budget
               Secretary
               Membership Committee
               CIVIC
               Reader-companion in nursing home
               Big Brother-Sister Program, Southside Youth Center
               CHURCH
               Choir
               Youth leader
               Sunday School Teacher

INTERESTS: Skiing   Music
               Chess   Dancing

An ordinary résumé can become effective when attached to a powerful letter.

83

Following are two résumés that pass the appearance test with flying colors. Let's see how they fare during a twenty-second scan and beyond.

Nancy Jones

Nancy Jones's résumé has arrived at the desk of a laboratory director who needs an assistant to help run a quality-control laboratory in a pharmaceutical company. With candidates far outnumbering openings in biology, the advertisement for the job has brought in hundreds of applications, and the director is wearily scanning them one by one to find the few that will be of interest to him. Conditions are not favorable for Nancy. She has to catch his eye with impressive qualifications or she is not going to get anywhere.

The director picks up Nancy's résumé. Immediately, he is impressed, because it looks attractive. He thinks the résumé reflects an orderly mind. Most résumés he has looked at just do not put it all together.

He begins to read. The job objective annoys him; it strikes him as being long-winded. Why couldn't she simply say she is interested in applied biology? What is this business about working with people? Is that there because she has doubts about biology?

If résumés are supposed to say only what needs to be said, what about this line?

Born January 6, 1964   5'7"   135 lbs.   Single   Excellent health

Does it say anything about her ability to do the job? The biologist doesn't think so.

His eyes move down the page:

Education   Iowa State University, Ames, Iowa
Bachelor of Science, June 1986
Major: Biology   Concentration: Physiology
GPA: 3.3 on a 4.0 scale

Major Subjects   Minor Subjects
Mammalian Physiology   Qualitative Analysis
Vertebrate Anatomy   Quantitative Analysis
Histology   Organic Chemistry
Genetics   Biochemistry

NANCY O. JONES

Present Address | After June 1, 1986
105 Belleville Place | 1212 Centerline Road
Ames, Iowa 50011 | Old Westbury, New York 11568
Phone: 515-924-6674 | Phone: 516-544-7119

Born January 6, 1964   5'7"   135 lbs.   Single   Excellent health

Career
Objective
Research and development in most areas of applied biology, with an opportunity to work with people as well

Education
Iowa State University, Ames, Iowa
Bachelor of Science, June 1986
Major: Biology   Concentration: Physiology

GPA: 3.3 on a 4.0 scale

Major Subjects	Minor Subjects
Mammalian Physiology	Qualitative Analysis
Vertebrate Anatomy	Quantitative Analysis
Histology	Organic Chemistry
Genetics	Biochemistry

Scholarships
and Honors
University Scholarship: $2850/year
Iowa State Science and Research Award

Dean's List two semesters

Activities
Volunteer Probation Officer, 1983–84
Probation Department, Ames, Iowa

Tutor, Chemistry and Math, 1983–86
Central High School, Ames, Iowa

Member, Kappa Zeta social sorority

Women's Intercollegiate Hockey Team

Special Skills
Familiarity with Spanish; PLC and FORTRAN computer languages; typing

Work
Experience
Teaching Assistant and Laboratory Instructor
Freshman Biology   School year, 1985–86

Waitress, Four Seasons Restaurant
Catalina Island   Summers, 1984, 1985

The résumé of Nancy O. Jones does not communicate her career-related experience.

She has used the outline form well, so he is able to take in a great deal of information in one look. She impresses him with her education.

Double spacing above and below her grade point average makes it stand out. However, if her average had not been quite as good, and if she had not wanted to feature it, she could have used single spacing to make it less conspicuous, like this:

Education   Iowa State University, Ames, Iowa
Bachelor of Science, June 1986
Major: Biology   Concentration: Physiology
GPA: 2.7 on a 4.0 scale

Now that she has told him about her grades and her courses she wants to drive home the point that she was no ordinary student. She flags him down with the headline "Scholarships and Honors," and he sees her financial aid and science awards, which make a favorable impression. Two times on the dean's list may not be important enough to set apart by double spacing, but it makes a modest impression.

Up until now, Nancy has made a favorable impression overall. The director is ready to take in the next batch of information:

Activities   Volunteer Probation Officer, 1983–84
Probation Department, Ames, Iowa

Tutor, Chemistry and Math, 1983–85
Central High School, Ames, Iowa

Member, Kappa Zeta social sorority

Women's Intercollegiate Hockey Team

She almost loses him by featuring her work as a probation officer. That is not of primary interest to him, but through good spacing and placement, she draws his eye to the next item, which states that she has tutored chemistry and math. Unfortunately, Nancy now loses him permanently by ranking tutoring along with the sorority and the hockey team. He guesses she has made her major statement about biology, and so he turns to the next résumé.

Good as it is, Nancy Jones's résumé could be improved by reorganization. Her tutoring in chemistry and her two years as a teaching assistant and laboratory instructor in biology reveal more than an academic interest in biology. They should be featured. Everything related to biology and any other information of possible use to the employer should be put under a new marginal headline and statement, as follows:

| Career-related Experience | Biology Lab Instructor and Teaching Assistant Freshman Biology (1985–86) |
| | Chemistry and Mathematics Tutor Central High School, Ames, Iowa (1983–86) |

Skills and Interests	Microscopy	Computer Languages:
	Electron Microscopy	FORTRAN, PL/1,
	Histology	COBOL
	Spectrum Analysis	Statistics
	Small-Animal Surgery	

Now, the director is able to see things she can do. "Good," he says to himself, "She can use an electron microscope. We need someone with that skill."

By no means should Nancy eliminate mention of the hockey team, but since she is applying for a professional job, the first bait to throw out is credentials; they testify to her ability to do the work. After that, what may sink the hook is how the employer sees her as a person. He may have picked out bits here and there that testify to her diligence, but the picking out depends on chance reading; it would be best not to leave anything to chance. With a slightly different presentation, she might ensure that he receives an impression of her diligence.

There are other areas she could strengthen, things she has underplayed or totally neglected to mention. Sticking the waitress job in down at the bottom of the page is almost an apology for it. She may also have had other jobs, such as baby-sitting, household work, or door-to-door sales, that she belittles in her mind and has not even mentioned. Mention of such things might make a good impression on an employer looking for somebody who is not afraid to work and who is mature for her years.

If we quizzed Nancy, we might find that she could put something like this on her résumé:

Scholarships and Financial Support	90% self-supporting through college as follows:
	University Scholarship: $2850/year Iowa State Science and Research Award
	Waitress, Four Seasons Restaurant Catalina Island (Summers, 1984, 1985)

Teaching and instructing, baby-sitting, home
maintenance, selling

And this, because her activities tell something about her as a person:

Activities   Volunteer Probation Officer (1983–84)
                 Kappa Zeta social sorority
                 Women's Intercollegiate Hockey Team
                 Skiing, sailing, singing, tennis

Double spacing has been cut down so as not to overemphasize the less important items, yet a string of other things not terribly important in themselves has been inserted to support the impression of an active, interesting person. Sometimes you want to leave an impression, at other times you want to emphasize a qualification. For example, Nancy wanted to feature her studies, and the way she brought them out by listing them in a column was good. If she had listed them like this, they would not have stood out:

Major Subjects: Mammalian Physiology, Vertebrate
Anatomy, Histology, Genetics
Minor Subjects: Quantitative Analysis, Qualitative
Analysis, Organic Chemistry, Biochemistry

On the next page, you will see the Nancy Jones résumé as she might have revised it to emphasize the strong points that would have been of interest to that director looking for a resourceful assistant. The added emphasis might have made the difference that would have landed the job for her.

Nancy's revised résumé is pure outline, devoid of prose. It works well for her. When she states that she has studied quantitative and qualitative analysis, and knows PL/1 and FORTRAN, a scientist reading her résumé knows what this means.

Janet Smith

Janet Smith, whose résumé follows, has a different problem in presenting her qualifications. She needs to *describe* what she did in order to tell an employer about her qualifications, so her résumé calls for a mixture of key words and prose to get her message across. Yet

NANCY O. JONES

Present Address
105 Belleville Place
Ames, Iowa 50011
Phone: 515-924-6674

After June 1, 1986
1212 Centerline Road
Old Westbury, New York 11568
Phone: 516-544-7119

Career Objective   Research and development

Education   Iowa State University, Ames, Iowa
Bachelor of Science, June 1986
Major: Biology   Concentration: Physiology
GPA: 3.3 on a 4.0 scale

Major Subjects	Minor Subjects
Mammalian Physiology	Qualitative Analysis
Vertebrate Anatomy	Quantitative Analysis
Histology	Organic Chemistry
Genetics	Biochemistry

Career-related
Experience
Biology Lab Instructor and Teaching Assistant
Freshman Biology (1985–86)
Chemistry and Mathematics Tutor
Central High School, Ames, Iowa (1983–86)

Skills and
Interests

Microscopy	Computer Languages:
Electron Microscopy	FORTRAN, PL/1,
Histology	COBOL
Spectrum Analysis	Statistics
Small-Animal Surgery	

Scholarships
and Financial
Support
90% self-supporting through college as follows:

University Scholarship: $2850/year
Iowa State Science and Research Award

Waitress, Four Seasons Restaurant
Catalina Island (Summers, 1984, 1985)

Teaching and instructing, baby-sitting, home
maintenance, selling

Activities
Volunteer Probation Officer (1983–84)
Kappa Zeta social sorority
Women's Intercollegiate Hockey Team
Skiing, sailing, singing, tennis

The revised résumé of Nancy O. Jones effectively features her career-related experience in a separate section.

prose can destroy the effect of an outline. The solution lies in imitating newspaper editors, who use headlines and subheadlines to attract readers. Like a newspaper, a résumé should lend itself to skimming, so the reader can quickly pick up a good overview of what is important. Then the reader can select specific things that interest him, and read further. There is an art to using headlines, but Janet Smith hasn't mastered it, at least not in the résumé she used to apply for a job with Hermann Langfelder, a hard-bitten old hand with thirty years in personnel and labor relations in the machinery business. He picked up her résumé and read:

CAREER OBJECTIVE	A challenging position in personnel administration requiring organizational ability and an understanding of how people function in business and industry.

That was pure baloney, and he choked on it. He thought of the hours he had spent in meetings, listening to a lot of hot air. "Challenging, my foot!" he muttered. Then he read the bit about her organizational ability and her understanding of how people function in business and industry. "I've been at this business for thirty years," he groused to himself, "and I still can't figure out how people function in industry. But *she* knows all about it."

Beware of Misleading Headlines

"Well, let's see what she's done," he said to himself, and then his eyes fell on "UNIVERSAL METHODIST CHURCH." That did it! He didn't want to bring any do-gooder into his factory to preach. He rejected her. And the fault was hers, in using the headline.

Janet's job at the church was administrative, not ministerial, and the church didn't care whether she was Jewish, Catholic, or agnostic. Only in its ministerial work does the Methodist Church need Methodists. But people—Langfelder and the rest of us—respond to symbols and make snap judgments on the basis of symbols. Janet had put the symbol of the church—its name—in a heading, when she could have done something better.

When you lay out your résumé, think of symbols. Imagine you are a newspaper editor who wants to put a story across. As an editor planning headlines, you must imagine yourself in the position of the reader. Ask yourself, "What words will catch the reader's eye? What words will put him off?"

JANET V. SMITH
111 Main Street
North Hero, Vermont 05073
(802) 772-4325

CAREER OBJECTIVE	A challenging position in personnel administration requiring organizational ability and an understanding of how people function in business and industry.
EDUCATION	PURDUE UNIVERSITY Hammond, Indiana Master of Industrial Relations June 1986 SMITH COLLEGE Northampton, Massachusetts Bachelor of Arts, Magna Cum Laude June 1981
WORK EXPERIENCE	UNIVERSAL METHODIST CHURCH 1 Central Square New York, New York 10027 Assistant Personnel Officer. 1983–85 Responsible for interviewing applicants for clerical positions within the organization and for placing those who demonstrated appropriate skills, for accepting and dealing with employees' grievances, and for developing programs on career advancement. CORTEN STEEL COMPANY Akron, Ohio 44309 Assistant, Personnel Office. 1981–83 Responsible for all correspondence of Personnel Director and for interviewing some custodial applicants and referring them to appropriate supervisors for further interviewing. BORG-WARNER, INC. Ithaca, New York 14850 Assembly linewoman. Summer 1980 Assembled parts of specialized drive chains in company with thirty other men and women.
COMMUNITY SERVICE	PLANNED PARENTHOOD North Hero, Vermont Counselor. Summers of 1978 and 1979 Explained various aspects of family planning and provided birth control information to clients of Planned Parenthood. Made referrals to other counselors and physicians where appropriate.
AUXILIARY SKILLS	French: Fluent. Knowledge of office procedures. Knowledge of IBM 360 Series.

The résumé of Janet V. Smith misleads the reader with irrelevant headings.

91

Use words that fit the job in question, and play down those that can lead an employer to think of you in terms that don't relate to the job. Ask yourself, "Does this say something to the employer?" Janet Smith missed the obvious. Her job titles would have made perfect headlines to attract Langfelder, and some of her duties would have yielded key words to send appropriate messages. The following arrangement would have been more effective for her:

WORK EXPERIENCE	ASSISTANT PERSONNEL OFFICER
	1983–85
	Universal Methodist Church
	1 Central Square
	New York, New York 10027
	<u>Interviewing, placement, grievances, and training</u> of applicants and employees in the clerical and support services of the church organization. Developed programs for the career advancement of employees.
	ASSISTANT, PERSONNEL OFFICE
	1981–83
	Corten Steel Company
	10 Lake Street
	Akron, Ohio 44309
	<u>Interviewing, referring, and correspondence</u> as an assistant for Personnel Director. Responsible for all correspondence and for interviewing some custodial applicants and referring them to supervisors for further interviews.

Let's suppose that Janet Smith has a chance to submit a second résumé to Langfelder. This time, she uses headlines that pinpoint the ideas she most wants to get across, so that he makes it past the Universal Methodist Church and gets down to the assembly line. "Hey, now, look at that!" he thinks. "She's worked out there on the floor. That means she's heard all the language and knows the gripes and the tedium. We have a lot of women in this factory, and it might be a good thing to have a down-to-earth, smart woman on my staff." (His sexism may have been showing, but this kind of employer is alive and kicking somewhere out there, and you may have to deal with him.)

What if Janet Smith wanted a job in the computer industry and had had ten years' experience with IBM? Employers are impressed by "graduates" of companies like IBM who are known as leaders in their fields. Ten years with them is significant. It might make sense to present her experience this way:

JANET V. SMITH
111 Main Street
North Hero, Vermont 05073
(802) 772-4325

CAREER
INTERESTS   Personnel Administration and Labor Relations

EDUCATION   PURDUE UNIVERSITY   June 1986
                   Hammond, Indiana
                   Master of Industrial Relations

                   SMITH COLLEGE   June 1981
                   Northampton, Massachusetts
                   Bachelor of Arts, Magna Cum Laude

WORK   ASSISTANT PERSONNEL OFFICER. 1983–85
EXPERIENCE   Universal Methodist Church
                   1 Central Square
                   New York, New York 10027
                   Interviewing, placement, grievances, and training of
                   applicants and employees in the clerical and support
                   services of the church organization. Developed
                   programs for the career advancement of employees.

                   ASSISTANT, PERSONNEL OFFICE. 1981–83
                   Corten Steel Company
                   Akron, Ohio 44309
                   Interviewing, referring, and correspondence as an
                   assistant for Personnel Director. Responsible for all
                   correspondence and for interviewing some custodial
                   applicants and referring them to supervisors for further
                   interviews.

                   ASSEMBLY LINEWOMAN. Summer 1980
                   Borg-Warner, Inc.
                   Ithaca, New York 14850
                   Factory work experience on an assembly line. Worked
                   with a team of thirty other men and women.

COMMUNITY   COUNSELOR. Summers 1978 and 1979
SERVICE   Planned Parenthood
                   North Hero, Vermont 05073
                   Explained various aspects of family planning and
                   provided birth control information to clients of
                   Planned Parenthood. Made referrals to other
                   counselors and physicians where appropriate.

AUXILIARY   French: Fluent. Knowledge of office procedures.
SKILLS   Knowledge of IBM 360 Series.

The revised résumé for Janet V. Smith stresses what she did rather than the less important point of where she did it.

EXPERIENCE: 1976–86
IBM Corporation
Binghamton, New York
<u>Assistant Personnel Officer</u>

Were she an engineer after a technical job that could use her IBM experience, highlighting the name of the company would have been a good idea. Imagine employers giving the résumé a twenty-second scan. What words should you use and how should they be placed to catch the eye and make employers want to read further?

Mark Meyers—The Functional Résumé

Janet Smith and Nancy Jones were lucky. Their training and experience translated into satisfactory headlines to highlight their experience, but that doesn't always work. Sometimes the only way to get a message across is to create a résumé based on functions. Mark Meyers, whose résumé follows, adopted that technique to help him get a job in community recreation.

When he began to write a résumé, he tried time and time again to get his message across in a conventional résumé in which he first listed his education, then his experiences in chronological order, and finally his activities, hobbies, and interests. But writing it conventionally raised all sorts of problems. He wanted to highlight his public relations and promotion experience, some of which he had been paid for and some not. Some of it had also been secondary to a primary assignment. Dividing up this experience and placing bits and pieces of it in various parts of the résumé to make it conform to a conventional style diluted its impact. Also, his athletic ability and experience would mean a great deal to an employer in his field, but how could he show it effectively? Some of it had been gained as a participant, some through training, and some as a coach. Could he expect an employer to sift through the various sections of the résumé to find out all he had done in athletics? (Remember, you can only count on an employer giving a résumé a quick scan before deciding whether or not to study it more fully.)

His solution, as you can see, was to feature the functions of the job he wanted and then describe things he had done that pertained to each area. Thus, under each function he developed the equivalent of a mini résumé.

MARK MEYERS

1414 South Harp Road
Dover, Delaware 19901
(501) 267-3087

CAREER INTEREST
Community recreation.

RECREATION PROGRAMMING EXPERIENCE
Planned and implemented programs in stagecraft and drama;
assisted with programming in ceramics, photography, and
physical fitness for Dover Youth Bureau summer program.
Summer, 1981.

Lectured and led tours at Atlantic County (Delaware) Park nature trail
and visitors' center. Prepared slides to illustrate lecture; helped in
construction of nature exhibits. Summer, 1980.

Coordinated men's intramural sports competitions for Hoboken
University. Had responsibility for equipment and scheduling.
1979–81.

PUBLIC RELATIONS AND PROMOTION EXPERIENCE
Directed publicity efforts of University Drama Club for several
productions. Developed innovative techniques—such as a
costumed cast parade to arouse interest in an avant-garde staging
of "Alice in Wonderland," which gained campuswide attention.
1979–80.

Advertised in various media and became familiar with advertising
methods, including writing news releases, taping radio
announcements, designing graphics for posters and fliers. Drama
Club, 1980–82; men's sports, 1979–82.

LEADERSHIP AND ATHLETIC ABILITIES
Trained in outdoor leadership and survival skills by Outward Bound.
Summer, 1978.

Coached hockey and basketball. Dover Youth Bureau, 1981.
Participate in hockey, swimming, backpacking.

RESEARCH AND EVALUATION ABILITIES
Prepared college research project on the recreational needs of
residents of a Hoboken neighborhood. Designed questionnaire to
solicit residents' own perceptions of their needs; interviewed
residents and local officials. Fall semester, 1981.

Reported on effectiveness of Dover Youth Bureau programming.
Summer, 1981.

OFFICE SKILLS
Dealt with unhappy and irate customers at McGary's Department
Store, Dover. Worked at service desk, tracking down problems
and rectifying errors. Summer, 1977.

Typing and use of office machinery.

EDUCATION
Bachelor of Science, June, 1982   Major: Recreation
Hoboken University, Hoboken, New Jersey   Minor: Drama

The résumé of Mark Meyers illustrates the functional style.

Preparing a Résumé for a Specific Job

Mark stated his case well, but you can't get blood from a stone. He found he had to look outside his field, because jobs in it were virtually nonexistent due to cutbacks in government funding. In his search, he ran across the following job listing from the publisher of a magazine for parents:

EDITORIAL SECRETARY

B.A. in Liberal Arts

Interested in childhood training. Well organized, outstanding language skills. Typing and clerical skills, potential to use electronic text-editing equipment. Reporting to Coordinating Editor, Happy Days magazine. Assist in all editorial functions. Evidence of creativity essential. Entry-level position with career potential.

Can you put yourself in his shoes, analyze the job, and devise a résumé that speaks to the stated needs of this employer? The clue to doing it is to go through the job description and step by step take your cue from the employer. Right off you will hit a bit of a snare because the employer has specified a B.A., while Mark has a B.S. His drama minor might give him appropriate credentials, however. If he shows his education something like the example below, it might reflect the liberal background the employer apparently prefers:

EDUCATION   HOBOKEN UNIVERSITY, B.S., 1982
              Major: Recreation   Minor: Drama
              Humanities courses:
              Introduction to Dramatic Literature
              British Drama to 1700
              History of Theater
              Playwriting
              Introduction to Poetry
              Shakespeare
              English History

Next, the job calls for an interest in childhood training, then language skills, and so on. Each specification suggests a headline for a résumé. Mark faces another stumbling block in being able to demonstrate an interest in childhood training, since his experience was only with older youths. Since a résumé makes points by stating facts, he cannot demonstrate an interest in childhood training in his résumé because he lacks the appropriate experience. However, he *can* describe his interest in the letter that usually goes hand in glove with a résumé. He has a good basis for doing it, because the field of recreation certainly has much to do with the entire range of human development from childhood on. He should be able to point out corollaries in his education and experience with the work being done in childhood training, and he could check a library for information about childhood training to help develop the corollaries. Above all, he should read the magazine and try to tie in as many of his experiences as possible with the purpose of the magazine.

With his interest in childhood training brought out in a letter to complement his résumé, he might then proceed to develop his outline as follows:

EXPERIENCE   HUMAN DEVELOPMENT

Dover Youth Bureau. Planned and implemented programs in drama, photography, athletics, health. Summer, 1981.
Research Project. Studied recreational needs of a Hoboken neighborhood. Interviewed residents, developed questionnaire. Project provided an insight into the family life and problems of parents in a neighborhood setting. Fall semester, 1981.
Outdoor Leadership Training. Practical experience in human development through a knowledge of nature and survival skills.

LANGUAGE SKILLS AND CREATIVITY

Writing. Wrote releases, developed advertising, and prepared radio announcements for Drama Club, men's sports programs, and other events. Wrote report on Hoboken research project. 1979–82.
Lecturing. Gave talks and led tours at Atlantic County (Delaware) Park nature trail and visitors' center. Summer, 1980.
Audiovisual. Prepared slides for audiovisual presentation for visitors' center. 1980.
Promotional. Created innovative techniques—such as costume parade of cast—to arouse interest in avant-garde staging of "Alice in Wonderland," which gained campuswide attention. 1980.
Design. Designed posters, fliers, and other graphics for sporting events, plays, and other campus events. 1979–82.
Constructed nature exhibits at nature center. 1980.

BRUCE GREGORY ROBERTSON

Home Address
105 Comstock Drive
Pierre, South Dakota 57501
(605) 257-7236

College Address
5 Erasmus Drive
St. Paul, Minnesota 55101
(612) 220-2020

CAREER
INTERESTS
- The marketing of products or services in industries such as banking, publishing, and retailing.

EDUCATIONAL
BACKGROUND
- Macalester College, St. Paul, Minnesota   A.B., May 1986
Major: English   Minor: Economics
Honors: Dean's List   1985–86

EMPLOYMENT
- Sales - Southwestern Publishing Company, Memphis, Tennessee.
Educational dictionary sales to families with high school pupils: summer 1984 in Santa Fe, New Mexico; 1985 in Asheville, North Carolina; assisted in training new salesmen.

- Administrative and Clerical - Temporary Help, Inc.
Typing and other business machine operations, bookkeeping, clerking, complaint adjustments; short-term assignments with auto dealers, banks, real estate operations, schools, and similar employers: summer 1983; part-time 1984.

- Miscellaneous - Camp counselor, stock clerk in grocery store, baby-sitter, newspaper boy. From high school on have earned money for clothes, travel, and purchase and maintenance of an automobile.

ACTIVITIES
- Vice President, Seven-Come-Eleven investment club
- Varsity basketball
- Coach and tutor, St. Paul Concordia Boys Club
- Debate Club
- Book and Bottle literary club

SKILLS
- Typing
- PLC and FORTRAN computer languages
- German: fluent

HONORS
- Dakota Interstate Scholarship
- Hubert H. Humphrey First Prize, Minnesota Intercollegiate Debate

INTERESTS
- Public speaking and debate
- Investments
- Writing
- Parachute jumping

A résumé designed more to reflect an active, energetic personality than specific experience.

CLERICAL AND ADMINISTRATIVE
Clerical. Typing and use of office machinery,
McGary's Department Store. Summer, 1977.
Administration. Responsible for equipment,
scheduling of programs, and coordinating of
competitions. Hoboken University, 1979–81.

The functional résumé allows you to develop a different message for each job, or type of job, you wish to apply for. Different functions can be highlighted, depending on what the job requires, and your specific experiences rearranged under different headings. It gives you the flexibility you need if your experience has been varied and diverse.

Bruce Gregory Robertson—A Résumé Reflecting an Active Mind and Body

Finally, there are merit employers who are interested in candidates not so much for what they know as for what they can learn. They want to see a résumé that reflects an active person with an active mind. Bruce Gregory Robertson is such a person, and he has designed his résumé as much to reflect his personality as his experience.

The Curriculum Vitae

A curriculum vitae (literally, "course of life" in Latin), also sometimes called a C.V. or vita, is a résumé for academic positions, and as such it does not need a statement of goals or interest. While there is merit in keeping nonacademic résumés brief by focusing on employers' needs, a faculty tends to select colleagues not just to teach, but for the prestige they will bring to the department, especially in the long run. An eminent faculty attracts eminent associates. Publications, research, memberships, and honors all contribute to telling what a candidate is like, hence long vitae that reflect many achievements are traditional. The same candidate in applying for an industrial position wouldn't list a raft of publications, for example, if those publications didn't relate to the job in question.

The following lists in a logical way all the essentials of a good vita. Note the correct way to list publications. In academia, those who list them incorrectly are jeopardizing their chances of being hired.

MICHELLE TRIO

Department of English
Athens College
Athens, NY 14850
(607) 123-4567

406 East Bates Street
Athens, NY 14850
(607) 654-3210

EDUCATION

Ph.D., 1979, Cornwall University.

Dissertation:	"The Anatomy of Sin: Violations of *Kynde* and *Trawbe* in *Cleanness*," directed by L. E. Cooper (DAI 40/09, p. 5046– A).
Major Subject:	Old and Middle English language and literature.
Minor Subject:	Medieval philology.
Courses:	Old English; *Beowulf;* seminars on the Junius Manuscript, the Exeter Book, and hagiography; Middle English literature; Chaucer; *Piers Plowman;* Medieval Latin; paleography; Old French; Middle High German; Old Icelandic; Dante.

A.M., 1974, with High Honors, Boston University.

B.A., 1972, *magna cum laude,* Honors in English, State University of New York at Stony Brook.

PROFESSIONAL EXPERIENCE

1980–present: Assistant Professor, Medieval and Renaissance Literature, Department of English, Athens College. Position includes: Engl 325 Chaucer, Engl 323 Triumph of English (a course on the history of English which I instituted), Engl 232 Medieval Literature, Engl 420 Shakespeare Seminar, Engl 231 Ancient Literature, Engl 107 Introduction to Literature: Myth, Legend, and Folktale.

1980: Assistant Professor, Department of English, Cornwall University Summer Program. One section in "Practical Prose and Composition" and training of a graduate teaching assistant.

1979–1980: Lecturer, Department of English, Cornwall University. Two courses in Freshman Seminar Program: "Shakespeare and Politics" and "Practical Prose Composition." I was Co-Director of the latter, with responsibility for planning the syllabus, training and evaluating graduate teaching assistants, and leading staff meetings on problems and goals of teaching composition.

PUBLICATIONS

"Heroic Kingship and Just War in the Alliterative *Morte Arthure*," to be published in *Acta,* 11.

Articles on the Beatitudes, the Handwriting on the Wall, the Parable of the Marriage Feast, Sarah, and Sodom and Gomorrah in *Dictionary of Biblical Tradition in English Literature,* ed. David L. Jeffrey, to be published by Oxford University Press and W. B. Eerdmans.

"On Reading *Bede's Death Song:* Translation, Typology, and Penance in Symeon of Durham's Text of the *Epistola Cuthberti de Obitu Bedae,*" *Neuphilologische Mitteilungen,* 84 (1983), 171–81.

PROFESSIONAL SERVICE AND ACTIVITIES

1. At Athens College
   1984–1985: English Department Library Representative.
   1984–1985: Member, Athens College Faculty Enrichment Committee.
   1983–1985: English Department Personnel Committee.
   1982–1984: English Department Committee on the London Center.

2. Elsewhere
   1980: Organizer and Chair, Latin Section, Northeast Modern Language Association. Topic: "Eschatology and Apocalypticism."
   1975–1977: Organizer and Chair, *Quodlibet:* The Cornwall Medieval Forum.
   Memberships in MLA, Medieval Academy of America, International Arthurian Society.

HONORS

Charles A. Dana Fellowship for Excellence in Teaching, Athens College.
Goethe Prize in German Literature, Cornwall University.
George Lincoln Fellowship in Medieval Studies, Cornwall University.
Teaching Assistantship, Medieval Studies Program, Cornwall University ("Medieval Literature in Translation").
Teaching Fellowship, English Department, Boston University ("Freshman Rhetoric and Composition").

LANGUAGES

Reading knowledge of Latin, Old French, Spanish, Italian, Middle High German, and Old Icelandic, in addition to the usual French, German, and Old and Middle English.

CREDENTIALS

Dossier may be obtained from the Educational Placement Bureau, Barnes Hall, Cornwall University, Athens, NY 14853.

The Job Objective

"Do I have to have a job objective?" According to my calculations, as of this writing I have been a career counselor for 2,028 weeks, and I have been asked that question at least six times a week, except for the 117 weeks when I was on vacation. When I answer, "No, I don't like the heading JOB OBJECTIVE," the sigh of relief is audible. The job seekers think I have let them off the hook for one of the most important parts of a résumé. I haven't. With rare exceptions, a résumé should open with an objective—it's the way it is phrased that can be changed.

I show them the preceding Robertson, Meyers, and Smith résumés and tell them that I prefer the headline CAREER INTEREST because it leads to a simple and direct way of stating the purpose of the résumé. For example, I suggest they try rewriting the Robertson and revised Smith statements of interest as job objectives to see if they don't find it awkward. After a struggle they come up with the kind of baloney found in the unrevised Jones and Smith résumés.

They listen politely. I may have helped them with a minor problem of phrasing, but I know that I really haven't dealt with their question. Then they tell me what I already knew: They don't want to state a goal because they don't know what they want to do. I ask them to imagine themselves as the employers reading their résumés. If theirs is like the revised Nancy Jones résumé that is so obviously slanted toward biology, then employers can figure out what the résumé is for without a stated objective. However, I wouldn't fool with a résumé that didn't tell me at the outset what it was all about. When I have to start studying a résumé to guess what the writer wants, I throw it in the wastebasket.

Next I point to the Zarote and Robertson résumés, which wouldn't make any sense without a statement of purpose. And I can't get up much enthusiasm for a letter as a substitute for an objective. A letter stating a purpose accompanied by a résumé without' purpose is a wasted letter.

I remember a young woman who, on short notice, got a chance to be interviewed by a recruiter from a large department store. Knowing very little about merchandising, she headed for the nearest department store, where several managers were kind enough to give her information and the loan of their trade journals. In three hours of investigation, her eyes were opened to an industry in which people pursued careers in training, employee relations, promotion, credit, public relations, merchandising, and other occupations. Several of these looked interesting, so thanks to word processing, she easily changed a few things on her résumé, then listed her objective as:

CAREER INTERESTS: Training, promotion, and public relations in a retail setting.

Like most of us, her range of aptitudes was wide, so like a chameleon she showed the recruiter only those that seemed to match retailing.

One Page or Two?

If a résumé can be kept to one page, so much the better. The length depends on the message. In reading résumés where everything is jammed on one page with none of the white space or headings that can make them attractive and readable, I have wearied of trying to find information and have given up. On the other hand, it has never been the least bit tiring to lift a piece of paper and turn to a second page while scanning an interesting résumé. A résumé is an outline. It needs white space. It needs headings that stand out. Don't sacrifice them for some arbitrary notion about one-page maximums.

Additional Advice About Résumés

No matter how you develop your message, test it before you send it to employers. Get friends to give you a critique of your résumé or vita, especially if they are in an occupation in which you hope to find a job. A word of caution, however. Unless you guide them, their critique may relate more to the ritual than to the message. One job hunter had modeled a résumé after Janet Smith's. The critic took a red pencil and put all the dates of employment in the left-hand margin. That would have been a good idea if it had indicated long years of experience with a company such as 3M, signifying considerable experience with one of the best-managed companies in the country. But the dates in question referred to short-time summer jobs, which were of no consequence to the message and cluttered the margin with information that distracted from the headlines.

One way to get a résumé criticized is to hold it up a few feet from the reader and ask for comments on its appearance. Does it look neat? Is the layout pleasing? Does it look easy to read? Is the print good-looking?

Next, give the critics the résumé to read. Let them make all the comments they want. You may pick up valuable ideas for improving its style and layout, but be careful you don't get caught up in inconsequentials. What you really want is to have your critics look at the résumé as if they didn't know you. You might even show them a résumé with an alias, then ask:

What qualifications does this person have?

What do you see this person doing with these qualifications?

What kind of an employer would want to hire this person?

Does the résumé project an image of a certain kind of person? What kind? Aggressive? Thoughtful? Energetic? What?

In other words, ask your critics the most important question about your résumé: "What message do you get about me?"

Chapter 7

Brainstorming for Unusual Careers

Don't follow the crowd of job applicants. Use directories to guide you toward interesting occupations that others don't think of.

What would you really like to do?
  What in the world is there to do?

- Music
- Sports
- Hobbies
- Politics
- Religion
- Business
- Art

These words are signposts that point to careers and lead you to people at work. Find signposts by reading directories.

When you become accustomed to using directories to research the thousands of activities that provide employment, you may find it hard to understand why so many people draw a blank when they try to think about what they would like to do. Nothing occurs to them!

Career planning has become too studied, too conventional, and too concerned with security. Almost everyone has had ideas about getting into some field, but invariably conventional notions about careers attack these ideas and all too frequently succeed in driving them back into the recesses of the brain, there to hide or die. Quick, before you can say, "I can't do that," write down the things that interest you. The more far out your ideas, the better; no one else may have some of your ideas, thus cutting the competition for jobs.

DIRECTORIES

Go to a library big enough to have Bernard Klein's *Guide to American Directories*,[6] a veritable atlas of careers. Run down the table of contents. There, you will find 338 broad headings, such as advertising and public relations, art and antiques, banking and investments, camps and camping, detective agencies, foreign affairs, lumber and woodworking, motion pictures, pollution and environment, travel, and urban affairs. All become signposts that point to careers.

Under each heading, Klein's descriptions of the directories provide still more signposts. For example, the heading "Consumer Affairs" covers organizations engaged in product testing and evaluation, consumer education, and assistance for people who have complaints about products or services. Some organizations are private, others are governmental. With a little imagination, the descriptions of directories can be transformed into an outline of consumer affairs occupations.

For another extensive guide to possible careers, study the *Directory of Directories*,[7] published by the Gale Research Company. Its extensive subject index guides the reader to directories listed under specific areas, such as "Air transportation industry–Freight" or "Air transportation industry–Passenger." People looking for ideas and sources of information will find that this book and Klein's complement each other.

Do Not Limit Your Investigations

If you really want to look into the nooks and crannies of the

American workplace, you will need more than directories. Could you, by chance, become interested in Esperanto, the universal language? There are people who believe that establishing a single language for everyone would avert worldwide misunderstandings and who have made the promotion of Esperanto their lifework.

What about doing something with steam-driven road graders, sawmills, threshers, or other types of machinery?

ASSOCIATIONS

How do you track down people in unusual fields—or even those who work in normal fields? Alexis de Tocqueville found an answer when he visited the United States in the first part of the nineteenth century. What he wrote then still holds:

> The Americans of all ages, all conditions, and all dispositions constantly form associations. They have not only commercial and manufacturing companies in which all take part, but associations of a thousand other kinds, religious, moral, serious, futile, restricted, enormous or diminutive. The Americans make associations to give entertainments, to found establishments for education, to send missionaries to the antipodes. Wherever at the head of some new undertaking you see the government of France or a man of rank in England, in the United States you will be sure to find an association.

Thus, the ultimate directory, the one with signposts to direct you to every imaginable career, is the *Encyclopedia of Associations,*[8] also published by Gale Research. In it, you will find out about the Rough and Tumble Engineers, an association of people who run those steam engines that may have caught your interest. If you think Esperanto could be your metier, the *Encyclopedia* will give you the names and addresses of six associations fostering the language.

Browsing through the *Encyclopedia of Associations* is like looking through a kaleidoscope of human activity. Any two people with a common interest always seem to find each other somehow and form an association. Once they do, you can find your way to them through the *Encyclopedia*. Every trade, business, and commercial interest seems to have an entry.

Are you considering a career working for your father or another relative? This is always a tricky proposition. Look up the Sons of Bosses International (S.O.B.'s) to discuss the problem with the membership.

Would you like to be a dowser? The American Society of Dowsers can tell you all about forked sticks, rods, and pendulums that help you find water, oil, or minerals, and it will give you assistance in using them.

If you have a desire to be a successful yacht broker, you can get ideas and information by looking up marine associations and then going to their members for information interviews.

In addition to being a fountain of ideas for careers, the *Encyclopedia* reveals information about associations that helps job hunters in three ways:

1. *By providing information.* The directory provides names and addresses of association executives, people who are good sources of information and contacts. Some associations distribute occupational information or publish journals that are sources of vocational information. Once, while collecting occupational information about health careers, a librarian wrote to various associations concerned with health care and received enough pamphlets on medical occupations to fill five large ring binders.

2. *By locating jobs.* Some associations, particularly those in the professions, provide placement services or set up placement booths at annual conferences. Many publish journals that feature job listings.

3. *By revealing interesing places to work.* Some associations are potential employers. Do you have a patriotic bent? The Daughters of the American Revolution employs 150 people; you could become one of its employees. Perhaps you could edit one of its publications, or you might get a job helping the organization administer its scholarship and loan programs.

If you have a strong religious belief, you might turn your zeal toward making a living working for a religious association. If I have added up the staffs of the various Bible associations correctly, 690 people are making careers promoting Bible studies, maintaining libraries, fostering scholarship, encouraging children to memorize parts of the Bible, translating the Bible into different languages, and searching it for a secret code used by the prophets.

Sports, hobbies, and fraternal organizations are fostered by associations. How do you feel about lawn bowling? Twenty people are working for the American Lawn Bowls Association on behalf of its 9,200 members.

If you are interested in lobbying for a cause, writing for a publication, arranging meetings, arbitrating disputes, running educational programs, giving speeches, counseling, doing public relations work, or just about anything else, browse through the

Encyclopedia of Associations. You will get many ideas about jobs and places to work.

I remember a college student quizzing me about careers in banking. Each question made me think, "I don't know what motivates this guy, but for someone supposedly interested in banking, his questions are off the mark." After some probing on my part, his true interest—horses—surfaced.

I suggested he consider a career in the horse industry. It is a multibillion-dollar business that includes racing, betting, breeding, showing, shipping, tack manufacturing and merchandising, publishing, government regulation, medical care, training, feeding, and grooming. (Until he was injured, my son-in-law shoed horses for a fee a physician would envy.)

I pulled out the *Encyclopedia of Associations* to show the prospective banker the many facets of the horse industry, hoping he might see the possibility of a career in something that interested him. We read about the American Horse Council, which was described as an organization of businesses and individuals with commercial interests in the horse industry. The council, we discovered, publishes the *Horse Industry Directory,* possibly a valuable source of signposts that would point to careers. In the *Encyclopedia,* the student spotted the American Quarter Horse Association, with its staff of 225 people engaged in promoting his favorite breed. For a moment his eyes lit up, and I hoped he would plan to contact people in this organization for information interviews. But he did not. How sad. Education should have given him the confidence to take a risk, to pursue an adventure, but apparently it had conditioned him to try to find a secure path.

He even lost out on having a good time. It would have been fun for him to look into the horse industry. To become more knowledgeable, he would have had to read the trade journals, which for him would have been pure pleasure.

BOOKS

What about becoming a writer? How about a career in the travel industry? Or in health care? For a guide to books on careers in these fields and hundreds more, see *Where to Start: An Annotated Career Planning Bibliography.*[12]

TRADE JOURNALS

What would you really like to do? The chances are there is a trade journal or a magazine covering something of interest to you. How about photography? Perhaps you'd like to run your own camera shop someday. Start reading *Photo Marketing Magazine,* published by the International Photo Marketing Association. You will read information about the latest products, ideas for running a photographic business, current marketing practices, and other news of the trade. You will get a vicarious experience that you may transform into the real thing. Take a vacation and call on photo dealers, once you have read enough to be able to speak their language. They will be delighted to meet a person who has made a hobby out of learning about their work. Who knows, you may meet someone who wants to be bought out in a few years.

Why do we think changing jobs has to be a matter of cutting off one job and starting another? Why do we think a career has to begin with a full-time job? Or even with a job? How grim for a housewife to sit in an employment office thinking she has no experience and feeling like a pariah. And feeling sorry for herself. She shouldn't. Her transfer from working at home to holding a job outside the home can be gradual, beginning with vicarious experiences. What could she look into? The industry serving artists, galleries, or collectors? What about importing? Or fashions? The travel industry might be interesting to her if she knew more about it. The place to start learning is the library. Books have been published about most industries, and trade journals provide information about current trends.

The best resource for identifying trade journals and other special-interest magazines is *The Working Press of the Nation,* Volume 2, *Magazine Directory.*[9] Since many trade journals are published by associations, the *Encyclopedia of Associations*[10] and the *National Trade and Professional Associations*[11] are also sources of information.

Directories, associations, and trade journals are sources for names. Directories usually give the names of key people in an organization, names of people to contact. Articles in trade journals also mention names you can use. Would you like to know the names of woodworkers near you who could tell you about their work? Write to the secretary of the International Woodworkers of America, who might be able to give you names of members in your area.

Chapter 8
Following Money to Jobs

Organizations that are on the move and expanding are the best prospects for jobs.

To find jobs, find industries, businesses, private institutions, and government agencies that are expanding. To find these organizations, follow money.

Bankers and investment counselors know about money. Ask one of them who is spending it. Or ask two.

Alternatives to "Go West, Young Man"

Lazarus was about to give up. His children were well established in the local schools, he owned a home that had been in his family for two hundred years, and he had a deep involvement in his community. When he came to see me, Lazarus was forty years old.

"So God knows, I hate to pull up stakes and leave," he told me, "but the whole region is economically dead, and it looks as though I'll have to move to where the jobs are."

Nonsense. There are always jobs around.

As the former president of the firm of Undershaft and Lazarus, Lazarus had sold his business to a conglomerate with the understanding that he and the rest of the work force would be kept on. It was soon apparent, however, that the new owners wanted neither him nor the workers, for they closed the factory, moved the operations south, and there, benefiting from lower taxes and cheaper labor, exploited the company's patents, markets, and reputation.

Lazarus's problem is similar to that of many others who choose their place to live before they choose their place to work—for example, the Wall Street executive who decides to kick over the traces, leave the rat race behind, and move to New England, or partners in dual-career marriages, where wives or husbands have difficulty trying to find a job reasonably near their spouse's place of work. And it is like the story of any graduate with a new degree coming back to the old hometown—an ever-so-humble hometown when it comes to finding jobs. In fact, Lazarus could have been any job hunter trying to make his way against bad economic headwinds.

He needed help.

Lazarus gave the impression that he had gone everywhere and tried everything. He cut me off fast when I first mentioned bankers as a source of help. He told me every banker in town knew him, and that he was, indeed, a director of one bank. All the key bankers had his résumé, which they had sent to the top business and industrial leaders within a radius of 40 miles. Could they do less for such an important man? And how could they do any more?

He had been introduced to all the corporation presidents he ever hoped to meet, and several more besides. Nothing had come of it, he said bitterly.

He did not need to give me any more details. I already knew what had happened.

Friends, friends of friends, business acquaintances, and business acquaintances of business acquaintances, out of sympathy, had given him an employment interview. But to a man, they saw him only as the former president of Undershaft and Lazarus, not as a potentially useful person. Like the housewife who couldn't get employers to see her as anything other than a housewife, Lazarus was stuck with a label. Lazarus stood in front of employers, hat in hand, seen as an *unemployed* president. Pathetic.

I can see him in the eyes of those employers. A charity case. Poor fellow. And the employer thinks to himself, "There but for the grace of God go I." Something must be done for Lazarus, but of course the employer can't use a president, or even a vice-president. What to do? Ah, yes. Help him with contacts. Line up some appointments for him.

I can hear the employer on the phone. "Bill, this is Chuck Jones from Consolidated. Do you know Harry Lazarus? Got kicked out at Undershaft and Lazarus. Very raw deal. Was president, you know. Awfully nice fellow. I wondered if you might have something for him?"

Bill is retrenching and doesn't need a high-level executive. He promotes from within (now that he thinks about it). Or he only takes on people with experience with gear-cutting machinery. And so forth.

"Well listen, Bill, I told Harry I would line up some appointments for him, and I mentioned you. Would you see him anyway? You may have some ideas for him. Thanks, Bill, you're a prince. Harry's awfully low. It will do him good just to have some interviews."

Bill meets Harry. Bill feels sorry for Harry. Bill lines up an appointment for Harry to see Catherine. Catherine feels sorry for Harry, so Catherine lines up an appointment with Jim. Jim lines up an appointment for Harry to see Susan, but Harry breaks it and goes to see Elmo, who runs a saloon. Harry gets drunk.

What went wrong?

Lazarus's introductions set him up as an unemployed president looking for a job as an executive—even though he was not especially interested in becoming a top executive. Financially, he had made out well selling his business, and he could easily have retired. He had even tried it for a while but found it boring. Being without a job had given him an appreciation of employment that all too few people have. Lazarus especially enjoyed working in finance, production planning, or purchasing—jobs that required planning or analytical skills. But neither he nor the prospective employers had thought to discuss management problems. The interviews never got around to examining any problems the employers may have had—problems in the areas of finance, purchasing, or other areas of interest to Lazarus. Lazarus should never have advertised himself as someone looking for a job. He should have started out with information interviews to discover the employers' needs.

When Lazarus was through telling me how hopeless his situation was, and after I had calmed him down, I got him interested in information interviewing and how it works for the job hunter.

I suggested that he return home, see his banker and anyone else to try to identify growth employers, and then proceed with information interviews. While I thought he might in this way find a suitable employer, I also had in mind what had happened to someone from

113

rural Vermont who was once in Lazarus's shoes. The Vermonter never did find an employer who could take full advantage of his previous experience, but he discovered a number of small firms that took him on as a consultant to help them solve specific problems. For him, it worked out better than having a full-time job.

Lazarus was skeptical that any employers in his hometown were doing well enough to hire anyone on any basis. Nevertheless, he went to his banker, this time for information.

Look at Needs, Not Job Titles

When he approached his banker for information about growth companies—organizations that might need help with growing-pains problems, and the possibility of consulting for such organizations—lights flashed in the banker's mind. "I never thought about employers' problems when we talked previously," the banker said. "All I could think of was who might need a president or at least a vice-president, and my mind drew a blank." The banker immediately mentioned one of his customers who had been complaining about a shortage of management talent.

One week later Lazarus telephoned me to say he had a job.

"Of all things," he said, "it's with a textile company, and I thought textile companies in this area had all died out years ago. I knew that somebody had bought the old Schwartz mill, but it's such a wreck of a place I never thought to call on them. When I went to see them after the tip from my banker, and started exploring their problems instead of mine, they just about fell all over me to get me to come to work for them. They don't know who has ordered what in their purchasing department, and that needs attention. They also need a study to see whether to fix up the old plant or build a new one, and they have a dozen other problems to keep me busy for years."

Naturally, I was interested to know why this one company was thriving while others in the same industry in that area were dying. The answer: it had developed fabric that was especially suitable for making heavy-duty winter clothing for skiers and snowmobilers. It was buried under an avalanche of orders—and Lazarus had found his opportunity.

Find the Employers Who Are Prospering

In the worst of times, in the best of times; in the most economically depressed areas or in boom towns; in depressed occupations or in healthy ones, there are always employers who are prospering, who are not struggling when others are—or who are running ahead of the pack in good times.

To find such employers, find the people who are investing in them or who are lending them money—*and pump them!*

Prospering and growing organizations need money to finance growth. Bankers, who make money by lending it, make it a point to find organizations that are growing and need to borrow. Organizations that are growing need talent. The point is made. Bankers are a source of information about the economy. You can't ask bankers to discuss their affairs, but you can ask them to name employers that are generally regarded by the business community as progressive and growing.

If you are more adventurous than Lazarus and are willing to follow money to growth companies no matter where they are—even if it takes you to Windy City or Dry Gulch—buttonhole a stockbroker or an investment adviser and ask about growth companies. Ask to see the financial reports published by Standard and Poor's and other investment services. Look up price-earnings ratios, the figures that reveal the price of a stock in relation to the per-share earnings of a company. Let us say you find that the shares of most companies can be bought at five times earnings—$25 a share, for example—but then you find that some stocks are being traded at fifteen to twenty times earnings and more. It may be that these premium prices are being paid because investors expect the companies to grow, like Digital, IBM, and McDonald's.

Large growth companies are listed on the New York Stock Exchange. For smaller ones, check the over-the-counter market and ask a broker what information he has on smaller companies. In other words, try to tap the resources of stockbrokers or investment advisers for information and advice. They can point out which companies the financial community expects to grow.

Ask your broker if she subscribes to an investment advisory service that attempts to identify budding growth companies. She may also have information on file for T. Rowe Price New Horizons, Lehman Capital, and Lexington Growth, three mutual funds that specialize in growth companies. Check where they are investing their money.

Look into the portfolios of venture capital investment corporations, such as American Research and Development. In a brochure, this company stated:

> The task of A.R.D. is to create, build, and develop new enterprises. It is a constructive effort which should be judged on a long-term basis. Our job is to study projects, the ones we conceive and the ones we receive, and then give all our help to those companies which we finance, hoping they will grow, mature, and provide A.R.D. with capital appreciation.

American Research and Development can afford to put a million dollars into a venture that may not work out because they may make many times that amount on another investment that does. Job hunters cannot hedge their bets that way; but they can diminish the risk by evaluating the track record of the venture capital firm and by selecting employers that are beyond the embryo stage and beginning to show a profit.

Profit is the key word. Look for companies with a consistent record of increasing profit, and you will undoubtedly find a good employer.

For guides to small businesses and other sources of venture capital, turn again to Klein's *Guide to American Directories*[13] to the section on directories containing information about private funds, opportunity-type investors, real-estate lenders, factors, and individual investors.

The more willing you are to move, the more valuable are these sources of information, since they cover the nation. For Lazarus and others like him—anxious to stay put—hometown banking friends are the best source of information, followed closely by real-estate brokers, especially those who deal in industrial, commercial, and institutional properties. Such people are ever on the alert for growing organizations that might need a nice piece of property to expand on. Insurance agents whose clients are businesses and industries have the same bird-dogging instincts.

People who sell sophisticated capital equipment, such as computers, telecommunications facilities, copiers, and numerically controlled machine tools, get a good view of managements and their use of the latest machines and techniques. Find an employer who is up to date in the use of sophisticated equipment and you will probably find a good place to work. Pump salesmen for what they know.

Money flows from the government like a gusher, and some of it may be coming to your community to create jobs. Because he would like to take credit for the funds that come into his district, your elected congressman, senator, or assemblyman makes it his business to know where funds are flowing, will flow, or are likely to flow to support a research project, build a hospital, or expand a service, any one of which would create jobs. Ask him where the money is.

Every contact you have can lead to other equally valuable sources of information. Do not hesitate to use them!

Chapter 9

If You Can't Get In the Front Door, Try the Back Door

If the path to the job you want is overcrowded or blocked, find another.

There are paths to doors of opportunity. Certain keys open certain doors. In broadcasting, you can easily find producers who will tell you that one key to getting started in their industry is to get a job as a secretary or a page. They can cite their own and other examples. In a professionally structured hierarchy, however, you would be hard pressed to find a former secretary or errand boy in a management position who would give you similar advice. Some employers prefer M.B.A.'s as management trainees, other prefer candidates with bachelor's degrees. Journalists seem to be split fifty-fifty over the merits of training in journalism versus training in the liberal arts. If you wanted a job as a reporter but didn't have the usual credentials, do you think you could get one? Here is how one liberal arts graduate did it.

The story of this quest ended with an editor saying, "You have no experience and less training, but you are long on brains and knowledge, and they are hard to come by. So you have a job."

The story began in the middle of Nevada as a young man drove his car west. His mind drifted back a few days to his graduation, then forward to San Francisco, but he mostly stared blankly at the emptiness of the landscape ahead. Boredom. And out of that boredom an idea popped into his head: he would get a job as a reporter on a San Francisco newspaper.

All he had was a B.A. with a major in economics. Even a degree in English might have made more sense. He had never so much as written a letter to the editor of the school newspaper. But he liked to write, and his professors had often said they enjoyed reading his term papers. "Yep, it's decided," he resolved to himself, "I'm going to become a reporter."

Before you hear the story of how he beat out hundreds of journalism graduates for the job he wanted, let's stop to think what you would do at this point. What ideas would you have in a situation like this? Information interviewing? It might work, but can you think of another strategy? It's time to pick up some other ideas.

Let's suppose that you are struck with an equally preposterous notion. One morning, while looking in the mirror, you decide you would like a career in the film industry or the theater. You have not taken courses in film or theater, nor have you done anything with an amateur group; in fact, you know very little about the entertainment industry. You would be competing for any openings with people who have dedicated years to preparing themselves for a job—some taking courses in school, others preparing via the apprentice route, perhaps taking tickets or shoving scenery around in a summer theater, anything for the chance to pick up a bit part. Considering the competition from such people, is it foolish for you to think of a career in film or the theater? Not if you offer secretarial skills, are an accountant, or have had extensive experience in financial analysis. Competent people who offer such talent are needed as badly in the entertainment business as elsewhere. Once you get a job with a company and become an insider, you have a chance to position yourself to take advantage of opportunities that may come knocking.

Did you have something more creative in mind, something more closely related to producing the show? It would seem somewhat unrealistic to suggest that you could walk up to the front door of a major producer and get hired, but stranger things have happened. Once, a major studio asked college placement officers to nominate candidates for an interesting job. The description began as follows: "We are looking for someone to replace Johnny Weismuller as Tarzan. The young man should have a luxurious head of hair, be over six feet tall, waist under thirty, hips ..." The last line? "Previous acting experience is neither necessary nor desirable."

Books on Specific Careers Are Often Useful

Never say that anything is impossible. You could walk up to the front door of a major producer and announce your candidacy for a role in the theater or film, as the case may be, but that door may not be open. If it isn't, try a back door or a side door. Better yet, figure out where the hidden doors are.

For the film industry, the task has been made much easier by the book *Getting into Film*,[14] by Mel London, one of those rare books about careers that is not only informative but readable. It expresses a philosophy about work and job hunting worth noting, regardless of the kind of job you want.

London identifies directories that are helpful. If you study these directories, you can see a film in the making. You see editing services, organizations that provide animation, film studios, equipment renters, talent agencies, experts on camera effects, renters of animals, food service organizations—these and other organizations whose services are brought together to make a film. You may not be able to work for a Hollywood studio, but even working for a company that provides food to film companies on location may be your back door to getting a foot in the industry. A job in advertising might serve as a side door.

Just as directories can be a source of ideas for careers, they can be useful in helping you see the mosaic of an industry. If I were trying to get a job in the aviation industry and I found the door to Boeing and the other obvious employers closed to me, I would take a cue from intelligence agents. I would study directories.

Like every industry, aviation has its ups and downs, and during one of the downs a design engineer with a major aircraft manufacturer was laid off. Applying to other manufacturers had led nowhere. All were in the same straits. A marketing directory gave him the idea to look into the users of the equipment he had designed; perhaps they might need him in the application and maintenance of the product. That did not work out, but it led him to a position as a purchasing agent for aircraft equipment.

Finding the Back Doors to Research

It may seem obvious that the designer of a product might find an opportunity with the user of the product, but our minds get on tracks. His was on two: design and aviation. When he dropped off the design track, he discovered other places aviation might lead him. He could have dropped away from aviation and pursued design. The

Research Centers Directory[15] published by Gale Research and the *Industrial Research Laboratories of the United States*[16] edited by Jacques Cattell Press are useful aids for engineers and scientists, especially so because they contain subject indexes.

During a difficult time for physicists, one physicist perused the Bowker industrial research directory under the heading "Ultrasonics," which led him to a laboratory using ultrasonics for fuel mixing, which in turn led him to investigate that field as an application he had not considered for a technique of interest to him. What opened his eyes the most, however, was the description of the laboratories, for it not only revealed research activities but also gave the number of staff members, their training, and their levels of education. He had been tuned to think of research as taking place in large universities or in government or corporate research laboratories—the kinds of organizations that were doing little or no hiring at the time—and he had no idea of the existence of small, more practically oriented research laboratories. He got a job with an organization staffed by people with bachelor's degrees who had no inclination to write research papers that would have gotten them known in more sophisticated circles. They were more interested in turning scientific theories into practical products for profit and were doing it with sufficient success to need additional help.

Finding All the Doors to Nontechnical Employers

No job hunters are more discouraged than the English majors who descend on *Time, Newsweek,* and *The New Yorker* every June, then come to the conclusion that jobs with magazines are difficult if not impossible to get. Most of them have not thought of investigating some of the biggest employers, such as McGraw-Hill, publisher of *Business Week,* and many other publishers of industrial magazines. The *Magazine Directory*[17] of *The Working Press of the Nation* includes information on over 5,000 publications, grouped under 188 categories, with 20 grouped under the heading "Exports and Imports," 19 under "Health Care and Hospital Management," and 19 under "Entertainment." If you are interested in magazine publishing, you might do well to consider a publication of special interest to you.

Ignored and probably unknown by most job hunters interested in publishing is the house magazine field, with its total circulation of 160 million—more than twice that of all daily newspapers, according to the *Internal Publications Directory,*[18] which is Volume 5 of *The Working Press of the Nation.* The directory includes information about the internal and external publications of more than 3,500 companies, clubs, government agencies, and other groups throughout the United States and Canada. Some, like Amoco's *Span,* have circulations in the thousands and would hold their own with good magazines on a newsstand because they carry articles of general interest, albeit about subjects relating to their businesses. Others, such as the *Morgan Guaranty News,* which is devoted to the internal concerns of that bank, its employees, and its retirees, circulate to a smaller audience.

It would be hard to estimate how many people are working for all these publications, but it must be in the thousands. Personnel attrition alone must be creating hundreds of openings every day. If the door is closed at *The New Yorker,* an open door at one of these other magazines is an entrée into the field. Fortunately, the directories include tables of contents and indexes arranged by subject, geographical area, and other breakdowns that help applicants develop a strategy for focusing their job-hunting efforts on a reasonable number of appropriate prospects.

Don't Think You Can't Do It

While the message of the ninth principle is "When traditional entrances to occupations are blocked, try the side door or the back door," it should also tell you this: Don't believe anyone who says "You can't." What they are really saying is "I don't know how to tell you to do it because I am not very imaginative."

When our would-be reporter arrived in the San Francisco area and started to look for his newspaper job, all he heard was "You can't." Let's pick him up where we left off and see whether he could or couldn't.

He and his friend holed up in Berkeley, which proved to be the staging ground for graduates planning to assault the San Francisco job market, as he told the story later, and just about every other one wanted a job as a reporter on a newspaper. Not only did most of them have bachelor's degrees in journalism but master's degrees as well.

"When I told them that I wanted a job as a reporter but had majored in economics, they thought it was the funniest thing they had ever heard," he told me later. "However, when I asked them how one *does* get a job on a newspaper, and they told me about writing letters, preparing résumés, and sending along clips, I knew how *not* to get a job on a San Francisco newspaper.

"Instead of following their advice, I went to city hall, to the police station, to the bars, to all the places reporters hang out. I found out what their papers wanted in a story. When news broke, I wrote my own version of what happened. I had the reporters show me around their newsrooms, so that I became familiar with the places. I went with them often enough so that the receptionists got to know me as a familiar face."

He went on to tell me how, just like a good reporter, he learned all about the editors and the publishers, their philosophies, their community interests, and the kinds of stories they liked. Then he picked up one vital piece of information: one of the reporters was leaving his job.

"I knew this fellow. I knew the kinds of stories he wrote, and I knew that he reported to the city editor. I knew the kinds of stories that the city editor liked, and I knew how to find my way to her office. I knew when she would be in her office, and I figured the receptionist knew me well enough that I might get by her if my visit seemed creditable. I tore up to the front desk with a sheaf of notes in my hand, said breathlessly, 'Gotta see the city editor,' took off for her office, barged in on her, and began talking a mile a minute. She started to laugh, and fortunately, we hit it off immediately."

Does aggressiveness turn you off? Generally speaking, I hope so. To be that pushy in getting to most employers would get you tossed out on your ear. Most of the time you can get to the person you want to see by writing or calling for an interview, by using a friend as a contact, or by some other less flamboyant tactic, but, as the fellow who told of this experience observed, "One thing I learned about reporters is that if they are going to get the story, they have to be pushy, so I knew it would not be out of character for me to be pushy."

And that is the point: *He learned.* He knew what he was doing.

You may think he stumbled on the job, that learning about a reporter quitting was an unusual break; but it wasn't. Things like this don't happen if you sit home and read the newspaper ads. But if you are out actively looking, you run across leads. Ask people how they found their jobs, and many of them will say they stumbled upon them; but in order to stumble, they had to be on their feet, going someplace.

Last year, a graduate began the rounds of importers, using the techniques of information interviewing. While waiting for her appointment with an importer, she sat down and started leafing through some of the notes she had made while doing her research on importing and exporting. Next to her sat an older man, also waiting for an appointment, who became curious and asked her what she was doing. She showed him her research notes, and it turned out that he, too, was in the importing business. He hired her.

Did she stumble into that job?

Opportunities come along by accident, but being ready and able to take advantage of them is no accident.

Chapter 10

When Opportunity Knocks, Do You Say, "Don't Bother Me, I Am Looking for Opportunity"?

Take a second look at all job possibilities. Don't assume you know what a job is about until you have studied it carefully. Investigate jobs that the crowd ignores.

In *Zen and the Art of Motorcycle Maintenance*, Robert Pirsig wrote that truth is often in front of us, but we do not see it because we are too busy searching for the truth. For job hunters, this translates into "Opportunity knocks, but you say, 'Don't bother me, I am looking for opportunity.' "

The tenth principle might be stated like this: To find an opportunity, look again at jobs you dismissed the first time around. Let me explain by telling you about M. Y. Opia, who graduated a few years ago to join the ranks of the unemployed for a long stretch until he finally landed a job as a clerk in a bookstore. There, if he had opened his eyes, he would have seen that he had an outstanding opportunity to learn the book business and to eventually buy out the owner. That he did not recognize his opportunity was not surprising given his track record extending back to college.

In his senior year, Opia and one hundred other students interviewed with IBM when that company recruited on campus. Along with just about everyone else in his class, he had also tried to get an interview with CBS, but the limited spaces on that schedule were given out by lottery and he lost out, as he did in similar lotteries with BankAmerica and AT&T. Dejected, he complained about the injustices of the system. He could have had interviews with numerous other employers who were scheduled to come to the campus, but they had canceled out because of a lack of student interest. The receptionist had tried to get M. Y.—and others like him—to sign up for an interview with American Hospital Supply, but M. Y. thought it was a diaper service for hospitals, so he dismissed the chance to interview with them.

Their job notice, which M. Y. had looked at but did not really see, indicated that this "supply" company *manufactured* and distributed over 6,500 items for health, educational, and scientific institutions. Successful candidates would be placed in a training program leading to positions in marketing, finance, and administration. An accompanying recruiting booklet, which he scanned but didn't read, contained a nugget that was solid gold for students who spoke a foreign language—which M. Y. did, having lived abroad for some years. Buried in the text was a hint that the company would like to hear from students with language skills for possible foreign assignments. It was not emphasized, because most organizations shy away from listing foreign openings, since they don't want to be inundated by students who think a foreign job would give them an opportunity to relive the summer they enjoyed bumming around Europe.

Finally, the booklet dropped this bit of information: "The health industry already is larger than the steel, oil, and chemical industries combined." This should have alerted M. Y. to the fact that this was a growth industry. If he had then pursued the matter and checked a few financial services, he would have learned that the company was a leader in its field. An annual report, which was given to him but which he left unread, revealed the company's remarkable record for growth in a variety of fields, including a service for planning, constructing, and equipping hospitals; a systems-planning service to improve techniques for handling supplies, laundry, food, and patients; and manufacturing, ranging from the production of hospital furniture to the production of artificial heart valves.

Some diaper service!

But instead of learning all this, M. Y. Opia had continued scanning the announcements that told him that IBM, Exxon, Hewlett-Packard, and Du Pont were interviewing. He salivated. Images of good pay, security, and prestige flashed before him. A job with a company like one of these was what he had come to college for. Hurriedly, he noted the names and stepped over to see the receptionist to make appointments to interview these employers, only to learn that they were interviewing engineers, which he was not. He was told to go back and look at the job listings again, only this time to read them. The receptionist suggested he check out Continental Grain, because they had openings for someone with his qualifications.

Continental's brochure, in words and pictures, portrayed careers in buying, storing, transporting, and merchandising corn, wheat, and other grains. Flipping through the brochure, looking at the pictures and once again ignoring the text, he saw pictures of farmers, good pictures if he had wanted to see himself in such a scene. But he wasn't interested in a bucolic life out in the heartland buying, storing, collecting, and shipping grain. He was more the city type. He never got to the pictures depicting the international nature of the business. Here was a chance for a career in a big city, dealing with traders in other large cities throughout the world. Here was a business where his knowledge of languages could have paid off. But once again, M. Y. barely touched the surface of the message.

Have you ever played word association, the game in which someone says a word and you respond with the first word that comes to mind? To Opia, "grain" created an image of pigs and hayseed, so he shrugged off the chance to compete for a job in a sophisticated, worldwide trading company.

Don't be misled by the name of the company—or to put it another way, regard a name like a face. Whether it is attractive or not so attractive doesn't tell you much about what is behind it. How would the trademark *American Standard* strike you if you saw it on a job listing? M. Y. saw that name at the head of a job listing, thought of plumbing, associated it scatologically, and turned away. Had he read the notice, he would have learned that the job was with a division of the company that had nothing to do with bathrooms. Furthermore, the company offered a management training program, which was just what M. Y. wanted.

Job listings are simply the sign on a door that you have to open in order to see what is going on inside. The trouble is that the doors are covered with mirrors that reflect our own preconceptions. Let's try you out. You have just looked at a job notice posted by an insurance company. What image did that create for you? Just based on the word "insurance," would you be inclined to read further? Did the word "insurance" suggest selling something that nobody really wants? That's the way a job notice from an insurance company struck M. Y. Opia. "What You Might See in the Insurance Business" was the heading. Underneath that was a statement that revealed that the company was in the surety bonding business, which they described in their notice as follows:

> Essentially, bonds protect one party from financial loss caused by the act or default of another. A bond covering public money construction—such as a school, hospital, or highway—guarantees the job will be done properly within the terms of the contract.

If M. Y. had not just glanced at the notice but read it and delved deeper, a new world of career possibilities could have opened for him—a world where he could have become an expert on construction, real estate, contracts, labor relations, and all other factors of mutual concern to contractors, builders, the public, and insurers.

"Insurance" in a word association game should bring such responses as investments, management, underwriting, investigation, real estate development, mathematics, and many other fields. For M. Y. the word meant sales, not even the sale of liability, fire, theft, or the many other kinds of insurance related to risk, but only life insurance sales.

M. Y. Opia was typical of the seniors who read the job listings in his college that year. What he ignored, others ignored. The jobs he applied for, others applied for. Someone from outer space, seeing these job hunters, would wonder what kind of crazy people inhabit our planet. They would see job hunters running away from available opportunities and turning to join a crowd pushing to get in where there were not enough opportunities to go around.

There is an Alice-in-Wonderland quality about job hunting. There is a looking glass on the door to employment that does reflect opportunity if you look for it, but the reflections most people see are their own images and concepts. To make matters worse, there are mirrors on employers' doors. They look in them to see the kinds of people they need, and they see themselves. Employers who graduated from state universities tend to see state university graduates as better workers than graduates of private institutions, and vice versa. The tendency of employers to pick applicants who reflect themselves introduces more nonsense in the already sufficiently nonsensical way the employment process frequently works. This is especially true for jobs where the criteria for success are based primarily on traits rather than training, such as those to be found in sales, advertising, and finance.

BE SKEPTICAL OF EMPLOYERS' NOTIONS

A few years ago, Mr. Black, of the investment firm of Black, Solder, and Company, contacted a few college placement directors at several colleges to ask them to refer candidates to his company for jobs in sales. In the course of the conversation with one of the directors, he happened to say, "Do you know the kind of young person I like to see get into this business? The son or daughter of a school teacher or a preacher. Someone brought up with fundamental values, who was raised in a family where there wasn't too much money. That is the kind of person I want. I was a preacher's kid." (Naturally!) He continued, "These are the kind of people who will work. The investment business has more than its share of socialite graduates who think that the way to develop business is to make contacts with rich clients over drinks at the University Club. I can tell you that those contacts are highly overrated."

As he spoke, the placement director thought of Lynn Wise, who fit the description of the sort of person Mr. Black wanted to a T. But when she showed up at Black, Solder, and Company, it was obvious that Mr. Black's notions were at odds with the hiring partner, a wealthy gentleman who didn't bring in much business but who was made useful in the personnel department. In a fatherly way, this personnel man advised Lynn not to get into the securities business, pointing out that she had no wealth of her own, nor did she know many wealthy people she could use for contacts.

With a shrug, Lynn dismissed Black, Solder, and Company and headed for G. I. Bicker and Company. A young partner in that organization had spoken before one of Lynn's classes about investments, describing the field as a wonderful one for women and confessing that she had made her first million before reaching her thirtieth birthday. To Lynn's surprise, the people at Bicker told her that she was too young for the business and suggested she start in a bank training program, get some financial experience, then come back after her thirtieth birthday. When Lynn pointed out that one of their partners was not yet thirty, the hiring partner simply blustered. No one likes to be confronted with the facts.

Unlike most job hunters, who tend to accept employers' opinions as wise counsel, Lynn saw the opinions for what most of them were— trite notions based on personal prejudices or, sometimes, she suspected, lame excuses for a brush-off. Listening to these opinions with a healthy skepticism, she went about the business of finding a job, estimating that she saw more than thirty employers before she got what she wanted.

Persistence like hers is to be emulated. Would that everyone had the self-confidence that wards off discouragement. In part, confidence like hers is internal, but a good share of it can be acquired through research. Before she began her job search, she investigated the field of investments thoroughly. When she called on employers, she had the confidence of knowing their needs and what she was after. Finally, she had shrewdness of a kind that helps guide you to opportunities. It, too, is a trait that can be acquired. To acquire it:

Learn not to trust first impressions. Take a second look.

Don't automatically follow the crowd. Look instead at what is being ignored.

Be skeptical of advice. It's usually given from a limited point of view.

In some ways, the tenth principle might be called the contrary principle. Job hunting takes place in a kind of wonderland, so when you see a sign pointing in one direction, read it again. It might read differently the second time.

Chapter 11

What's a College Degree For, Anyway?

Don't let pride or prejudice keep you from considering an unlikely job. What you can make of it—not how it looks to others—is what counts.

There is another mirror in our lives, the mirror on the wall. In it we see ourselves—our hopes and our fantasies. To make these hopes and ambitions a reality, our mirror must be turned to take in the world of work and moved around until we find a place where we fit into the picture. That is not easy to do, because we tend to try to find where we will look the best, not where we fit the best.

What we see depends on what we want to see. We tend to see occupations in terms of whether they will confer prestige and security upon us, not whether they offer us a possibility to *earn* prestige and security. We tend to disregard facts and respond to symbols. "The Establishment" is a symbol. Occupational titles are symbols.

If I suggest to you that selling is something you ought to consider, what is your reaction? Positive—you feel you are aggressive and would like dealing with people? Negative—you are not pushy enough? Or perhaps something more subtle is at work. You may not really be looking for compatible work at all but rather thinking in stereotypes. Because the word "salesman" does not symbolize something you want to be, you may not even be able to entertain the idea. You want to be a professional man or woman so you will be above the crowd. Never mind if the work would not suit you and your life would be dull. Sometimes occupational titles and what they symbolize lure people into work that proves disappointing, although it is not the pied piper effect of the glamour professions that is worrisome. You can work your way out of a bad situation. What bothers me are people who are not getting anywhere and won't look at the ugly duckling jobs because of fear of what taking such a job would do to their image.

To make this point, I often tell about a swan I know who owns a prosperous lumber and building materials store in a college town, located in the mountains beside a lake, where he and his family enjoy prosperity, skiing, sailing, concerts, sports, and the intellectual activities generated by the college. This is no Camelot, but it's close. His business prospers, which gives him a position of importance in the community, and as an educated person, he uses his position to foster educational, cultural, and recreational programs that enrich the life of his community.

Invariably, the story whets the appetite of the listener because it is about the good life—prosperity, family, and community service. Then, when the listener discovers that the business is a hardware store, the listener's enthusiasm deflates a bit. Then, when I mention that the hero of this tale started his career as an ordinary salesman, he becomes the ugly duckling for most listeners.

I remember using this story to counsel Ralph Gardiner. Let me tell you about him. His parents were the kind who labor long hours at difficult jobs to scrape enough money together to send their son to college—and, they hoped, to law or medical school. When Ralph was a teenager, he worked in the afternoons after school, on Saturdays, and during his high school vacations as a mechanic for a Lincoln-Mercury dealer. While he was in college, he worked there again as much as he could to help pay his expenses. By the end of his senior year, he had done just about everything for the dealer—sell, run the office, manage the parts department, repair cars. One summer, he actually ran the place while his boss joined an expedition to climb Mount Everest. Naturally, Ralph had an offer to join the dealership permanently after he graduated, an arrangement that would lead to a partnership if he lived up to his promise—and probably to another dealership offer from another automotive company. Companies like General Motors usually discover people like Ralph, find a town that needs a Chevy dealer, offer them the spot, and lend them the money to get started.

So what was Ralph doing in my office seeking career counseling? He already had a career in the automobile business. When we discussed the lives of the dealers in town, Ralph agreed that there was nothing wrong with being in their shoes, but he was hung up on the notion that his college degree was supposed to open the door immediately to some loftier career. Besides, his mom and dad would be disappointed if all their sacrifices had gone for "just" selling cars. Also, in the background was a prospective father-in-law, a prominent dentist who let it be known what he thought about owners of small businesses. Ralph was determined to show the old goat by getting into law school or becoming an executive trainee with a well-known firm like IBM, but these goals were eluding him. He had taken the Law School Admission Test, but his grades were too low for law school. He had been able to have many interviews on campus, but he had a dozen letters from the large and prestigious corporations, all of which began, "We have looked over your application very carefully and while we are impressed with your qualifications, unfortunately we have nothing to offer you at the present time that would do credit to your excellent talents." With law school out of the picture, and corporations in the meritocracy finding other seniors more meritorious, he wanted me to tell him what to do.

"But Ralph," I said, "you have your opportunity in the automobile business."

"I did not have to go to college for that," Ralph replied. "I could have done it right out of high school. How will it make use of my education?"

Poor Ralph. That question, "How will it use my education?" was the tip-off to a deep-seated bewilderment. Ralph had received an excellent education, but he did not know how it related to his career.

Our educational system often offers both education and training without distinguishing between the two. It's as if the system were educating centaurs, offering education for their human head, to impart a sense of direction and purpose, and training for their horse-like rears to make them useful workers. Ralph was attending a liberal arts college where he was being offered an education, but, thinking he was getting "training," he applied the courses to his rump. Now he needs a better head. He needs wit and wisdom. He needs imagination. He needs to be able to see himself in the abstract and work out a plan for making his way in life.

In trying to help Ralph see his opportunity, I used the story of the lumber and building materials store owner because it was apt, but with a slight twist of the plot I could have told him about the manager of the town's largest brokerage firm, who started as a typist, or a bookkeeper who became a banker. I could look around any community and find successful merchants, contractors, government officials, and businessmen who started in ordinary jobs, yet moved ahead. Still, to suggest a similar start to someone today would bring out the question, "How would that use my education?" The answer depends on how you define using an education. When I view the life of a community, I see libraries, parks, urban redevelopment, housing for the aged, schools, music and the arts, and the political scene. Then I see things being done, or not being done, depending on the biases of those contractors, insurance salesmen, merchants, and politicians who control so much of the town. "Movers and shakers," they are called, and it fits. I see the owner of a gasoline station becoming the mayor of the city, but I do not usually see the administrators and managers of Standard Oil in a position to put their jobs on the back burner while they became mayors, legislators, and commissioners. If Ralph had been employed, as he had hoped, by a large organization in the meritocracy, he would have "used" his education by giving his all to something like the accounting department of General Cosmetics. But by selling cars, insurance, or real estate, to name three possibilities—or by simply running a gas station—he would be on a springboard that others have used to jump to ownership of their own business and from there on upward to become the "movers and shakers" in the political, economic, and cultural lives of their communities.

You may feel that you are getting a sermon to convince you that it is better to start your career as a bookkeeper or a salesman rather than to put on a grey flannel suit and commute to the corporate headquarters of the First National Bank in the heart of a metropolis. Not on your life! I know that when you lock onto a notion of what you want to be, I might as well talk to a stone wall. But I also know that, like Ralph, you may not be selected by some prestigious corporation. You may not be admitted to law school. In the meritocracy, many are called but few are chosen. My message is, when the roast beef you expected is served to someone else, then go after the stew meat, put in your own seasoning, and lace it with some homemade wine. You can come up with something unique and far more satisfying than the standard fare on most career menus.

We put the wrong emphasis on jobs. We worry about what the job will do for us when we should be thinking about what we can do with the job. The best home builder I know of started as a carpenter's helper. It isn't what happens to you that matters, it is what you do about it. Do you remember the sad story of Brunner Wengen who lost everything—his job and then his wife? When the rug was pulled out from under him he went into a long tailspin, but he finally landed on his feet in Idaho selling ski boots. Getting out on the slopes lifted his spirits. One of his customers who owned a ski chalet in the area asked him if he would be interested in living in the chalet during the off-season as a way of protecting it from burglary. Brunner got interested in the problem of security, began to sell burglar alarms, and offered a maintenance and security service to chalet owners. He picked up a run-down chalet of his own, fixed it up, and, during the season, moved to a room in the basement and rented out the main part of the house to skiers. He began buying and selling other chalets, then a motel. Brunner Wengen is no longer an engineer. He is a real-estate tycoon.

In sizing up a job, look beyond labels and investigate the ingredients. Employment counselors, I am afraid, turn job hunters away from worthwhile careers by giving them labels that stereotype: salesman, auditor, insurance agent, administrator, designer—names that don't tell a thing about what you would be doing or what you would be trying to accomplish. It's the converse of the candidate who presents himself or herself with labels that suggest nothing useful to an employer.

The Reverend John Simonson's case was a classic example of how an ideal career was almost missed because an employment counselor came on too fast with a job title that, for John, symbolized what he did not want to be. He did not want to be a greedy businessman, pushing people into buying things they didn't need. He did want to be of service. He did need more money than his sparse and spare congregation could or would give him. The arrival of his sixth child underlined that fact. Listening to all his problems and questioning him about what he liked to do, the employment counselor listed the ingredients that would make up the kind of job Simonson would like and determined that:

1. It was important for Simonson to work for an employer whose product or service helped people in time of need. He would do well doing good.
2. Simonson should be able to select the customers himself who needed his product or service.

3. He had the self-discipline to manage his own time.
4. He needed a job where he could earn a substantial income.

In the counselor's mind, all of this added up to Simonson's selling life insurance, but instead of going over the ingredients and building a case, he blurted out the words "life insurance sales" and hit Simonson right in the cerebrum with an unfriendly symbol, temporarily closing the case on selling insurance. But something happened to make Simonson look past the symbols.

The message came via a parishioner whose husband had just died, a poor widow who would have been a rich widow if her late husband's partner hadn't cheated her out of half of the business. According to the surviving partner, he had tried to be fair; the widow claimed otherwise. However, the fact was that Simonson had a distraught woman on his hands who needed help.

In the process of talking to her, he learned that the two partners had once considered taking out life insurance on each other, with the premium to be paid by the business as an expense before taxes. At the death of a partner, the insurance would have been used to buy out the deceased partner's widow, taking care of her fairly and leaving the surviving partner unencumbered by an unproductive partner. Simonson became interested. Knowing of others in the church who might face the same situation, he got a life insurance salesman to talk to a Wednesday-night supper group about the ins and outs of insurance, social security, pension plans, and retirement benefits. The meeting was so successful and interesting that Simonson left the ministry and went into the insurance business, happily surprised that the financial angles of insurance and the way it could be used to affect taxes intrigued him perhaps even more than its social value. He had had no idea the field would offer him so pleasant a mental challenge. Many times, people who have had to change careers—for example, from teaching, when there are few teaching jobs available, to business—are surprised to find their new work interesting and very different from their expectations.

Simonson is now a man to be envied. His family prospers. He has the means not only to do right by them but to help with church work as well. His is a mobile career. When his wife took a job as a psychiatric social worker in another state, he had no trouble moving and reestablishing his business in a new community.

Very well and good, you say, you might not mind the lifestyle of a salesperson, but you don't want a job where you have to be aggressive. That's fine. Let's look at a publisher's recruiting brochure and see its description of sales:

Our college travelers cannot be pushy as that would only irritate professors. No salesperson can talk a professor into using a text if it does not suit him. Furthermore, one of the principal duties of college travelers is to solicit manuscripts. A good traveler becomes something of an expert in a field and knows when the time has come for a fresh text. Discussing books with professors, learning of their needs, and determining whether they have a manuscript in the works or whether they might like to submit a proposal for one is no time for arm twisting. We need representatives interested in education and in publishing; we do not need the stereotyped salesman.

The representative of a large rubber company, who called on manufacturers to sell them industrial rubber products, such as high-pressure hoses and gaskets, said that she never had any trouble getting to see a purchasing agent or anyone who might use the company's products. The products either fitted the manufacturers' needs or they didn't, so the art of persuasion hardly entered the picture. Although new products had to be explained, much of that was done with technical literature. The quality of the product was a matter of its manufacturer's reputation. Approximately four manufacturers made similar products, equal in quality to the ones this representative sold, but she sold more than her competitors, not because she had any better personality, not because she was more aggressive, not because she entertained, but because she gave service. When she took an order, she didn't just fill it out and send it in, she followed up on it to make sure it was sent on time. Once, when a small but important part was shipped incorrectly, she got in her car and drove 300 miles to get the right part for her customer (and to raise cain with the shipping department). "I don't sell," she said, "unless you call it selling when I am on the phone to our own people back at the plant to make sure they take care of my customers. I won't let my company let them down, and that is how I get the business."

Sometimes a salesperson is not a salesperson—or at least doesn't sell directly to the consumer. Procter & Gamble makes soap, and it employs "salespeople," but have you ever had anyone sell you a bar of soap? You *buy* soap. I like the way a woman I know who came here from Russia described the process. She said, "I go into a store and everything is so mixed up—piles of things, packages, red packages, little packages, all kinds of packages, all of them mixing me up. Then I see something that made the loudest noise on TV, and I buy it." Advertising did the selling, yet a salesperson, working with the grocer to ensure an adequate supply of soap in the store, was crucial to the process.

To ensure that their products are displayed properly, Procter & Gamble salespeople must vie for prime shelf space (none of this business of letting grocers put the products down on the bottom shelf out of view), organize special displays (pile the stuff up high in front of the cash register), and convince grocers to feature the products in their Wednesday-night newspaper ads. While the salespeople are fighting for their products, their competition is also fighting. It takes an aggressive salesperson to fight the battle in the consumer products business. But, because supermarkets are big business, and store managers are no longer glorified clerks who can be pushed around by salespeople, the job is changing. A modern grocery store is a million-dollar enterprise employing seventy or more people. Its manager probably thinks in terms of computerized inventory control, profit-center accounting, personnel development, and community relations. They are professionals, and a salesperson who can't meet a store manager on the level of one professional to another is in the wrong line of work.

The eleventh principle makes the point that pride and prejudice can prevent you from seeing an occupation for what it really is. Selling was used to illustrate the point because it is a many-faceted occupation employing enormous numbers of people. Yet the interest in it is proportionately lower than for other fields offering comparable challenges. Other occupations are similarly affected by a lack of understanding of what they really offer.

How many frustrated artists and writers are there, do you suppose, who could find working in an advertising agency creative and exciting but choose instead to work in a field such as teaching, where they are neither happy nor effective? By teaching, they feel that they are loyal to their principles. But what principles? The principle that they should disdain something they know nothing about? A principle of haughty attitudes? Attitudes, they are the problem. Even if some people took a job in advertising, they might feel that they had so lowered themselves that they would never be able to apply themselves and become successful.

If you follow reason's route, you can arrive at the door of opportunity, there only to find yourself unable to open the door because of your attitudes. We all see things through a kind of attitude lens, and you may not be able to see what you should see because of something in the lens that needs adjusting. It may be family traditions and pressures, peer-group influences, hero worship, ambition, vanity, sour stomach, the need for security, or any number of other factors that make up an attitude lens. When your attitude lens won't let you see the value in what reason has led you to, then check the things that make up your attitude lens.

Chapter 12

Making It Happen: A Review and a Plan

To help you decide what to do and how to do it, work up a written plan.

Thus far the aim of this book has been to give you insight into the world of work. It has tried to help you become wise to the wiles and ways of employment. It has proposed that careers and job hunting be considered three dimensionally—what needs to be done, your ability to do it, and the profit to be derived from doing it. To reinforce your ability to think three dimensionally, read the Introduction again, comparing the task of job hunting to General Motors' efforts to make a profit.

Like General Motors, which sets profit objectives, you too could benefit from outlining goals. Objectives can serve as catalysts, spurring you on to find the best possible opportunity. Use a loose-leaf notebook—loose-leaf because job hunting is a metamorphic process and you will be making changes and additions. Start with a page for your objectives, leaving space between each for future use. If the following happened to be the list of objectives of importance to you, and you received an offer from Merit Inc. and another from Ocean Treasure Hunters, the space would allow you to evaluate and compare the merits of the two opportunities.

Objectives

Prosperity, security:

Service to mankind:

Adventure, excitement:

Prestige:

Challenge and stimulation:

Satisfaction from filling a need:

Working conditions, compatibility of associates:

Location:

Other:

Remember that you will be hired because you can fill a need and someone likes you. To make that happen is a matter of marketing. Your immediate task, therefore, is to develop a marketing plan.

As described in the Introduction, marketing is a matter of landing a customer for what you have to offer, the same kind of challenge facing General Motors. Before that company lays out its plans for winning customers, it tries to anticipate the needs and likes of potential customers, then it targets its sales efforts to that segment of the market it can serve best. What it targets depends on what it can produce, therefore it must assess its capabilities—and so should you.

CREATE A TALENT INVENTORY

Unlike General Motors, locked in to its production capabilities, you are not limited by machines that can only put cars together. When you need to be analytical you can be analytical, persuasive when you need to be persuasive. You can get a haircut and wear a new suit. And, you can adapt in more than one way. One engineer innovates, another copies and refines; each gets the job done.

You have so many capabilities there is no end to the number of potential customers for your talents. Keep in mind, however, the lesson in the Preface about the language of employment. Employers may interpret capabilities differently than you do. Since they have the jobs, try to see yourself in their light as well as your own. Moreover, two lights illuminating your capabilities will help you discover many more things you can do than you ever imagined.

Review Chapters two and three, recalling the suggestion that you prepare an autobiography that will highlight traits employers can put to use. Create an inventory of your talents. Here are exercises to help you get started:

I. Describe what you have done that illustrates your:
   a. analytical abilities
   b. ingenuity
   c. persuasiveness
   d. leadership
   e. efficient work habits
   f. ability to organize programs
   g. ability to organize the efforts of people
   h. ability to express yourself orally and in writing
   i. integrity and loyalty
   j. tenacity in completing a task
   k. energy level

     l.   assertiveness

     m. imagination and creativity

   II. Review what you have done well, e.g., organized a ball club and recruited players, used ingenuity to develop a computer program, completed well-written reports, or found a cheaper and better way to make something. You may do better with this exercise than the one above because it is easy to dwell on things that gave you the satisfaction of accomplishment. In other words, "Tell me about yourself. What are your strengths? Your weaknesses?"

Next, list your experience or the skills you have acquired through training. One person might list machine design; another, credit analysis; and another, arbitrage. In other words, what can you put on your résumé?

Does your college or university, church, or community offer a career program incorporating self-assessment exercises? If so, take advantage of it. It helps to begin a career exploration and a job hunt knowing as much as possible about the tools in your tool box. Check out *The Complete Job-Search Handbook,* by Howard Figler, an invaluable aid in creating a skills inventory, and of course there is the famous *What Color Is Your Parachute?* to help you decide where you want to land. But most of all, learn about yourself and keep adding to your inventory of talents as you pursue your career exploration and job hunt.

CONDUCT MARKET RESEARCH

What you can do is only half the story; what you end up doing depends upon a need for you to do it. Analyze the market. Fortunately, it is so vast that you can begin by thinking about what you would like to do. (The inspiration for some of General Motors' finest products came from designers who dreamed up a car they would like to make.)

Turn to Chapter Seven, Brainstorming. Note its proposition that interests in almost anything—horses, recreation, rare books, politics, photography—are signposts to careers. Review the suggestions for identifying signposts. A career commitment based on an interest is both satisfying and a good omen for success. In the notebook you started, open a page and let yourself go. Write down the things that interest you.

You might find it helpful to consult a vocational counselor skilled in the use of tests who could help you identify areas of competence and potential interest. But if inspiration doesn't strike, if you don't find yourself hooked on music, or medicine, or the circus, and if your relatives are hounding you because they think you ought to know what you want to do, don't worry. Let other motivations give you a sense of direction.

Could you get interested in making a fortune? Review Chapter Eight, noting resources for finding growth industries and companies. If a company looks good and happens to be in retailing, learn about retailing and go after a job with that company.

Or perhaps you can't wait to get out of the old burg and you are looking for adventure. What about the travel industry, consulting, or diplomacy?

Fields

One way or another pick some fields that look like fertile soil for planting your seed corn, then identify and record sources of information that you can use for an investigation. Follow the example below of C. Darrow Seward, who decided to look for a lay career in religion and developed a page in his notebook like this:

Information Resources

Field: RELIGION

Information sources

Associations:
1. National Association of Ecumenical Staff
2. World Council of Churches
3. World Gospel Crusades
(Of course you would also want to record addresses, names, and information about the associations)

Directories:
Directory of Religious Organizations of the United States (Wilmington, N.C.: McGrath Publishing).

Books and Pamphlets (from *Where to Start: An Annotated Career Planning Bibliography*):
1. John Oelson, *Opportunities in Religious Service* (Skokie, Ill.: National Textbook, 1980).
2. William Gentz, *Career Opportunities in Religion—A Guide for Lay Christians* (New York, N.Y.: Hawthorn Books, 1979).

Trade and Professional Publications:
1. *Crusades Bulletin,* bimonthly publication of World Gospel Crusades.
2. *Ecumenical Review,* quarterly publication of the World Council of Churches.

Recruiting Literature: None identified

Personal Contacts:
1. The Reverend Wesley O'Toole Moses

Occupations

Whether in government, business, or eleemosynary institutions, whenever organizations get much beyond twenty-five or more people, functions such as personnel administration, purchasing, public relations, marketing, office management, security, and sales become formalized occupations, thereby creating trait-oriented job possibilities for smart people.

Does the notion of a career in personnel administration strike a chord? If so, don't go charging out to talk to employers before you have learned what it is all about. Personnel administration is an occupation comprising many functions. Which ones interest you and why? You tell an employer you would like to be involved in training or employment interviewing. You are told that new hires in the personnel department start in salary classification. Do you think you could do that job? Develop an information resource card much like the one you would develop for a field and follow through with an investigation, and you will become able to handle the questions.

Remember the U.S. Bureau of Labor Statistics' *Occupational Outlook Handbook,* a major source of occupational information. I couldn't be without it, although I hope you look more imaginatively at occupations than does this plodding handbook. Also, read it and any other broad-brush forecast with skepticism. The overall outlook for an occupation or industry might be rosy, but even an industry as booming as the computer industry has its pockets of depression.

Read trade and professional journals and business publications for current trends. Anyone who tries to pick a trend by putting faith in statistics and forecasts without finding out what is behind them is headed for trouble.

People Resources

There is no resource like people. Make a list of friends and acquaintances and note what they do. Howard Carroll tapped his relatives and friends for contacts, but what if you are new in town? In the Postscript, note the story of Court, the Contact Man. In Chapter Eight, note the people who are likely sources of economic information.

OCCUPATIONAL AND EMPLOYMENT RESEARCH

Literature Search

Having identified resources, read before you head out to talk to people for information and advice. It's difficult if not impossible to conduct an information interview if you don't know something about an occupation. Develop an outline along the following lines:

Information Notes

Field or occupation:

1. Purpose—What need does it fill and for whom or what?

2. How does it accomplish its mission? Organizational structures, occupational and job descriptions:

3. Personal experiences, traits, and skills that relate to the occupation:

4. Occupational challenges—problems and difficulties that have to be overcome to achieve results:

5. Industry and occupation trends:

6. Profit prospects, pay scales, outlook:

7. Employment information—career paths:

8. List of potential employers:

9. Other:

Relative to point three, as you read, be alert to relationships between your own and your prospective employers' needs, especially for trait-oriented jobs. Keep a pencil handy when reading trade and professional journals. Watch for articles or remarks about problems and trends. If a problem is discussed, note the abilities required to solve it. For example, note the promotional ideas that helped launch a new venture, the patience and tact used in a negotiation, the astuteness behind a financial deal. Put yourself in these situations. Try to relate your experiences to them. Think about where you might have done well, and where not so well. Some are jobs to be sought, others to be avoided.

Note the names of any people mentioned in articles whom you may want to interview. Add their names to the page in your notebook where you are recording information resources.

Note: for an occupation such as sales where there are many different types of sales, or for an industry such as the music business, which comprises many activities, make a page for each subdivision. That will keep you from stereotyping work and help you sort out the niches and find those that best suit you.

Employer Information

As you learn more about occupations, you will want to begin to focus on specific employment possibilities. From your reading and the notes you have made in your information notes from contacts, directories, and your own observations, start a page in your notebook for each potential employer. You will need a full page for each because, for employers of considerable interest, you may find yourself wanting to collect information as extensive as the following:

Employer Notes

Name of organization: _____

Address: _____

Phone: _____

Employment contact: _____

Type of business, industry, or activity: _____

Merit employer?_____

a. If merit, realistically, how well can I compete for jobs? _____

If no merit entrée for me, are there other side doors to get a job with this organization (Chapter Nine)?

b. If an American Traditional employer, what is its path to employment (apprenticeships, internships, experience, training, nepotism, etc.)?

---

c. Does the employer do most of its hiring through an agency, and, if so, which one? _____

Job description for position of interest: _____

_____

_____

Information Contacts:

a. For confidential inside view of organization and job that interests me, e.g., a person doing the kind of work I am after: _____

b. Former employee, person in another organization with a similar job, someone else with useful information about the organization and the job of interest to me: _____

---

c. "The person who has the power to hire me:" _____

Evaluation of the organization: Financial soundness, reputation in community, reputation of its products or services, employee morale, labor relations history, work rules, wage scales, growth potential, history of innovation: _____

_____

_____

The corporate culture (M.B.A. dominated, tuition assistance, values and ethics of coworkers): _____

_____

Special considerations: travel opportunities, chance of a job for my spouse: _____

_____

Review Chapter Two, for possible interview questions.

_____

Information Interviewing

When you have acquired enough information to make you occupationally conversant, and you have begun to develop extensive notes on selected employers, it's time to combine your library research with a field investigation. Reread Chapter Five, paying special attention to the seven points Carroll covered in an information interview.

Initially, information interviewing should concentrate on vocational information; later it can focus on specific employers to uncover needs you can fill. Note that at first Carroll interviewed employers for whom he didn't think he would like to work.

In your research, and as you conduct information interviews, strive to put yourself into the mind of the employer for whom you want to work. Make a list of things you would want someone who worked for you to accomplish and what you would like him or her to be like. Write a job description for the job you want. When you have done this, your research is complete and you are ready to begin your job campaign.

THE JOB CAMPAIGN

Résumés and Letters

In contrast to the standard practice of preparing a résumé as a prelude to planning a job campaign, the better practice is to prepare it when you can tailor it to the needs and likes of specific employers. Before you did much market research you may have already prepared a résumé. If so, read it again. Review Chapter Six and design résumés and letters that tell potential customers for your abilities what you are like and what you can do for them.

Also review the strategic considerations described in Chapter One. Recall that merit employers put as much or more emphasis on what you are like and what you can learn as they do on what you can do and what you know. Robertson's résumé, illustrated in Chapter Six, is essentially a merit résumé.

Other employers respond best to a résumé like Mark Meyers' that, point by point, matches qualifications to job requirements. With the aid of your notes, try to develop a functional résumé for each of the fields or occupations you researched. If it proves difficult because you can't directly tie your experience to the job, note Lance Zarote's letter and work up a letter that tells your story.

Priorities and Strategies

By now you have assembled considerable information, including the names of potential employers, hundreds possibly. Many of them never attracted you sufficiently to put much in your notebook beyond the name of the organization, its address, and the name and title of an employment contact. Don't discard these pages. Put them together in your notebook in a section labeled "C," indicating little interest. Create a "B" group for those of interest, but distance or other factors keep you from giving them your full attention. Finally, identify an "A" group to include those employers on whom you want to concentrate your best efforts.

While the "C" group doesn't appear to be of much interest, choose some to "test-market" your interviewing skills and other strategies. And who knows, you may get a tantalizing job offer.

For the remaining "C" employers, work up a form letter with an attached résumé and do a mailing in the spirit of advertising. Word processors make it easy to include a personalized salutation instead of the useless "To whom it may concern." Once you have worked up a letter to one employer in a particular field, you can send the exact same letter to a hundred others in the same category. Marketing yourself through this kind of "mail-order advertising" isn't the most productive way to find a job, but who knows? You may get some serendipitous responses.

The "B" group deserves more attention. Try to get interviews with them. Your letters will have sentences like this one to Dr. Smith, a chief chemist:

In discussing the work I have been doing in analytical chemistry, Professor Jones suggested that I write to you about the possibility of employment in your . . .

Or this:

I am planning a trip to Chicago during the week of June 10th and would like to call on you . . .

And this to a purchasing manager:

I have been investigating purchasing as a career possibility. My reading on the profession includes . . . and I have talked to . . . Ms. Anna Lytical of the Association of Purchasing Agents remarked that the way I went about investigating purchasing reminded her of the professionalism exhibited by agents as they do their research. Because I am interested in purchasing factory equipment she suggested I meet with you to talk about . . .

Finally the "A" group. Before his military service, Carroll struggled through a "B" and "C" job campaign. After his military service, he brainstormed, used information interviewing, and developed a résumé based on employers' needs. He test-marketed his interviewing techniques; he read books on job hunting. He did an "A" job of job hunting. His is the model to follow for the pursuit of "A" employers.

The Time Factor

The time between initial career exploration and the successful completion of a job campaign can take as little as a few hours, or it can take months. Twice times a few months is not inordinate for someone changing careers or pounding the pavement trying to get started on a career following graduation. Carroll's story in Chapter Five took place over four months of investigation, developing a network of contacts, and interviewing.

Graduate students in the humanities and social sciences who are forced to change careers because of the academic job market should prepare themselves mentally for an extensive job search, especially when they hope to find an alternative career compatible with their cultural and intellectual inclinations. For the most part, their career exploration and job search can't begin until they have completed graduate work, an uncomfortable situation because it's in their tradition to line up a position before they receive their degree. A job hunt can take as much time as writing a thesis. Since there aren't thirty to forty hours in a day the two can't be done at the same time. While still students, there is time for a certain amount of career research in the library, and it doesn't take much time to send off an application to a government bureau or research institution that happens to list a job. Academic administration or counseling can and should be investigated on campus without too much effort. But a truly extensive job search takes time, money, and the freedom to travel.

Money and Morale

Job hunting is draining financially and emotionally. Chapter Four outlines suggestions for coping with the strain, and Chapter Five illustrates how Carroll made his career exploration interesting. In the Postscript, read "Brother, Can You Spare a Cup of Coffee?" for a story about financing a job hunt and a reminder that temporary employment can be a way to find permanent employment while earning.

ALTERNATIVES

In success stories, so often the hero or heroine is someone who landed on our shores, penniless, ambitious, and energetic, but lacking a degree from an American college or university certifying their know-how. Unless a candidate is wearing a cap and gown, employers can't tell who is smart and who isn't. The golden door of Merit Inc. is not open to the tired, the poor, and the tempest-tossed except for jobs as floor sweepers. No matter, they will take the job. They are willing to work. Soon they may own the company. We read of one who started an ice cream company, another who started as a cobbler and now owns a prosperous shoe company. It could be that if these people had gone to an American college they would have acquired attitudes that might have kept them from taking the path they did. Like Ralph Gardiner in Chapter Eleven, they might have become like so many college graduates who ask "How can I use my education?" when they should be asking "How can I use my intelligence?"

With that chapter in mind as well as Chapter Ten, try to imagine yourself as a smart and ambitious immigrant. Free your mind of any notion of a career that would do anything for your ego other than allow you to become successful. Think about what you might do to make your way in the world. Look beyond yourself to people and their needs and try to identify needs you feel could be filled in some entrepreneurial fashion. The purpose of the exercise is to stimulate your imagination to get you thinking about work in new ways. You may come up with interesting ideas, yet choose not to pursue them because the potential profit in terms of self-esteem and security is insufficient—especially if the risks are great. Even so, the exercise will have served to put your values in clearer focus. But who knows, you might come up with some interesting ideas for a career you might never have thought of.

Chapter 13

Adjusting Your Attitude Lens

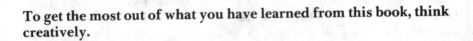

To get the most out of what you have learned from this book, think creatively.

If this book could accomplish just one thing, I would have it free minds of stereotype career thinking. We all see things through an attitude lens and there isn't anyone whose lens doesn't need a clearer focus.

In one way or another, all eleven principles, stated at the beginning of each chapter, relate to attitudes. You should try to understand yours so you can adjust your attitude lens to see the full range of opportunities available to you.

The first principle, in many ways, is an attempt to get college graduates to see why they are so tuned to the notion of a meritocracy and the professions. It is hard to get them to see otherwise. Education conditions them to see it as a track to the future, and everyone would like to be on that track. It's a matter of security. People do not like to start out on their own without knowing where they are headed.

Test yourself. Would the following kind of career be satisfactory for you? You live in a way by your wits. In the morning you give private music lessons. The demand for them is such that you could have pupils all day long, even though you have raised your prices far above other teachers'. You pursue your interests as a naturalist in the afternoon and have become something of a travel agent and arranger of tours for amateur naturalists. You are under contract to a publisher to produce a series of guides for naturalists, and you have another contract with a local museum for a series of lectures. You have a do-it-yourself career. Is it a real career or not? The real person in this case thinks not. He wants a career, like the one he had as a high school teacher, in which he can apply his educational background. Unfortunately, his school closed. Now he is investigating returning to college for a degree in accounting or computer science as a track to another secure professional career. Part of the problem is his wife, who has a profession and simply can't relate to a do-it-yourself career. It is very important that your spouse be able to adjust his or her attitude lens to yours.

Principles two through nine develop employment strategies that can be summed up as "find a need and fill it." To be able to see beyond yourself is a matter of attitude, an attitude that is hard to develop because job hunting by its very nature is highly personal. It won't help to just put "I want" into the attitude lens. For proper focus, the attitude lens needs a proper balance of "I want" with "employers need." Many people seek career counseling as a way of finding themselves. This book is not intended to be a counseling guide. However, if it were, the essence of its guidance message would probably be: To find yourself, lose yourself in something; become needed; try to focus your attitude lens on something outside of yourself.

Principles ten and eleven relate to attitudes and concepts, and these have their roots in history. As Marshall McLuhan has pointed out, "Most men are alive in another time, but you have got to be alive in your own time." Except for a few of the newer occupations, such as computer programming, occupational titles are anachronisms that bring forth images from times past. I say "salesman" and you think of Willy Loman, the salesman in *Death of a Salesman*," but the salesman I have in mind is a respected investment counselor who helps executives develop their investment portfolios. I say "grocer" and you think of someone in a white apron bent over a fruit bin, but the person I am thinking of, if bent over anything, is bent over a computer terminal to read the latest sales data. What these people are doing today, however, means less than what will happen tomorrow; that will determine where opportunity is to be found. It is hard enough to anticipate the future's challenges with the clearest of vision; it is impossible if your vision is colored by outdated values.

However valuable you may have found the principles, I hope the book has been more for you than a listing of shoulds and shouldn'ts. Each person has to develop his or her own successful style and system of job hunting. I hope that the stories in this book about other job hunters will give you ideas you can use and will help you avoid some mistakes.

"I'm a great believer in luck, and I find the harder I work the more I have of it."

—*Thomas Jefferson*

Postscript
Ten Who Got Jobs

By now you have realized that there is no one "right" way to get a job; counselors like me are always learning new ideas from the creativity and desperation of the job hunters they meet. To illustrate the fact that there is always a new twist, here are more ideas from people who actually got jobs.

I. The Stuntman

My car radio was tuned to a Toronto station. Being interviewed was Kenneth Waissman, who, along with Maxine Fox, produced the show *Grease*. I heard the interviewer say: "You and Maxine Fox produced a hit show when most people your age who want to get into the theater were probably off in some graduate school trying to pick up credentials in the theater arts to use as tickets to a job. How did you get started?"

I turned up the volume. This, I wanted to hear. Waissman mentioned sending résumés to producers. I turned up the volume again. Was I hearing what I thought I was hearing? A résumé campaign to get a job in the theater seemed to me the least effective strategy he could have employed. Waissman went on: "I must have sent a hundred résumés to each producer. I bombarded them with résumés. Nothing happened." ("Of course not," I chimed in, as if my voice could get through to them.) "When that didn't work," Waissman continued, "in exasperation I took a pinking shears and ran it right up through the middle of my résumés and sent them out again with a note attached: 'If you want to see the other half of me, I am available at your convenience.' It was a stunt, but it worked. I got a request for the other half that led to an interview and a job."

Don't count on this sort of gimmick to get a job, but don't just dismiss trying a strategy because it goes against conventional advice. And like Waissman, don't give up.

II. The Producer

Following her freshman year at Boston University, Maxine Fox got a job as a gofer in a summer theater outside of Baltimore. ("Go for some thread. The leading lady's costume just ripped." "That lamp on the table in the third act is all wrong; go find something better.") In Maxine Fox's case, however, it wasn't so much "go for." If there was a rip, she would see it and be ready with the needle. If someone put a contemporary lamp in a 1920s scene, she would hunt up a Tiffany lamp. When the box office was running behind, she was there to help. There was nothing obsequious about this; no toadying to a producer just to get a job. She was interested in the plays. She was interested in the business side of the theater. She was interested in seeing that everything went right. She lost herself in her job. And she was sure to be found. At the end of the summer season, a producer asked her if she could postpone returning to college for the fall term to help in the production of a play scheduled to open in the fall in New York. She was on her way and never returned to college.

Never underestimate the possibilities in a menial job. You may impress someone who has the power to advance your career.

III. The Contact Man

Court Cheval read about information interviewing and decided that it was just what he needed. His father had been in the Army, and his family had always lived on military bases, so Court knew very little about civilian careers. He needed to call on employers for advice and information, but he had no contacts; nor could he see himself getting them by using the methods he had read about in books on job hunting. They didn't suit his personality. He needed friends he could call on, so he decided to make such friends. Since he was already in Denver and liked the city, he decided he might as well start there. He already had a start because he had begun to attend the Presbyterian Church.

Instead of just attending church, he became active in church affairs by participating in a study group, helping with church suppers, and working with young people. He enjoyed these activities and began to meet people who were in business, social work, and government. He also moved into other activities outside the church, such as helping to coach Little League sports, working on a book sale for the local library, and doing volunteer work for the historical society.

To support himself, he did odd jobs, such as housecleaning and chauffeuring for a family he learned about through his minister. Because he was a hard worker and a likable young man, he soon had enough such work to keep him busy twenty-four hours a day.

Through the friendships he made in his church and civic activities and his various odd jobs, he had all the contacts he needed. He never really had to use them. He made such a good impression on several of his associates and employers that they began to ask him about his future plans. Soon he was offered and gladly accepted a position as the director of a youth center, a job for which he was admirably qualified.

IV. The Phoenix

The phoenix is a man who became a successful businessman, a philanthropist, and a leading fund-raiser for his college. At the time he graduated, he looked for a job for a while and had some good offers, but then he decided to knock around for a year "doing his own thing." The year stretched into several years. He traveled all over the world, hitchhiking through Europe, surfing in California, but he found his life had become very boring and aimless. He decided that he wanted to find a career, get married, and reestablish the upper-middle-class life he had known with his parents. The girl that he wanted to marry loved him, but she would have none of him until he proved that he could settle down and earn a living.

The young man and I met for the first time after he had been fruitlessly searching for a job for one month. He was devastated. The employers who had once made him substantial offers after his graduation now wanted no part of him. For the first time, he realized he was a bum, and no employer needs a bum.

In recent years, especially after the Viet Nam era, the phenomenon of dropouts who want to reenter what they once scornfully called "the establishment" has been fairly common. Their success has been limited. Employers are suspicious of people who avoid work. Moreover, for many dropouts who have had the desire for a comeback, some inner fabric seems to have been weakened.

I had to know the story of this man's comeback. I will let him tell it to you in his own words:

"As you know, I was a bum who had nothing to offer an employer. One did take pity on me and gave me a job, but it turned out to be wrong for me and for him. After years of having my own freedom, I simply could not settle down to the discipline of a regular job. Now I realize that no one could give me self-esteem; I had to earn it.

"One day, my car gave out, and I tried to con a used-car dealer into selling me one on credit, but he wouldn't do it. I needed a car badly, and I felt very dejected. I started to leave, when the dealer called me back. 'Hey!' he hollered. 'Sell some cars for me and earn one for yourself.' Of course, there was a hitch to the deal. He would not let me sell cars at his lot, because that would have been unfair to his regular salesmen, but he said it would be another matter if I could find people who needed cars and bring them to the lot.

"I talked to a couple of mechanics and found out the names of several people who had cars that were on their last legs and not worth fixing. Then I found good used cars to sell to them for less than it would have cost them to get their old clunkers repaired. Soon I had my own used-car business, then a new-car dealership, and now I have a string of dealerships. I also have a wonderful wife and three great kids, and you can be sure I won't let any of my kids bum around after college!"

V. The Trojan Horse

The scene was one of those college career panels where honored alumni return to tell students how they made it to the big time. One of the panelists was a woman who was a producer for one of the major television networks. The first question from the floor was, "How did you know what you wanted to do when you were in college?"

She answered, "When I was in college, I did not have the vaguest idea of what I wanted to do. I majored in English because I enjoyed it; then when I graduated, I went to the Katharine Gibbs School, because I knew that college graduates with secretarial training could get a job almost anywhere, and what I wanted to do was work in San Francisco.

"With my training, I had no trouble getting job offers. I picked one with a large insurance company as the secretary to an executive high up in the hierarchy, where I could see what went on in the hub of the organization.

"After two years, I had a much better idea of what the work was all about, who did what, and which jobs mattered and which didn't. I decided to take on New York City next. With experience added to my training, I knew I could get a good job almost anywhere, so I thought the television industry might be interesting. All three major networks offered me jobs. One was as the secretary to a top TV personality, a job I might have grabbed before I had worked in a large organization and found out what such a job would be like. I saw myself arranging his trips, making arrangements for his wife to meet him at various places, answering his mail—becoming his Girl Friday but practically never seeing him. There was another opening, however, a job as the secretary for someone who was creating a new children's program. The network had never done such a program before, so the project was starting from scratch. I knew that a secretary in such a situation would be in the thick of things and that with the right boss, she could work on the program, not just for him. I took the job, and it worked out that way. Before we were ready to go on the air, my boss was transferred to another project. I knew the most about the show, and I had proved that I could handle things. I took on his job, and from then on I was a producer."

VI. Chutzpah

The job looked good. The newspaper advertisement said to reply to a box number in Palo Alto. "That's a pretty good job," the man thought, "and I know that hundreds are going to apply. Palo Alto isn't all that far away. I think I will go there and try to figure out who the employer is. Perhaps I can find the mailbox listed in the advertisement and stand by it at the post office to see who picks up the mail." He did, the employer picked up the mail, and the candidate stepped up and introduced himself. He might have been the best candidate anyway, but his initiative made a good impression on the employer and helped him get the job.

VII. The Neophyte

It makes sense for neophytes in the job market to get over their awkwardness by first approaching employers who are not high on their list. After their techniques are sharpened, they can then take on places where they really want to work. The neophyte in this story had heard this advice, but she couldn't wait. She had to barge ahead and seek an interview at the one place she wanted to work most of all.

The interview was a disaster. She was awkward and inarticulate. All she could say was that she really wanted to work for the company, but she could not say what she could offer in return. She was turned down flat.

159

As she interviewed more, she got the hang of it and began to get some job offers, but her first interview gnawed at her. It had been for the job she really wanted. Figuring that she had one zero from that company and that two zeroes would not be worse than one, she called on the employer again, explained that when she had been there before it had been her first interview and that she had really not known how to handle herself. She told the employer that she really felt she had something to offer and asked if she could have another interview.

The employer was impressed. He liked persistence. The fact that the candidate had come back demonstrated a real interest in the company. A second interview was granted, and the young woman got the job.

VIII. Brother, Can You Spare a Cup of Coffee?

"I can't take time to find a job. I have to have one right now. I am broke." This is a situation familiar to many. Job hunting is expensive! One person found a partial solution to the latter problem. To see all the employers on his list of prospects, he had to cover fourteen states, so he bought a bus pass that gave him thirty days of unlimited travel, a place to wash up (the bus station), and frequently a place to sleep at night (the reclining seat of a bus). Rugged yes, but where there is a will, there is a way.

I have known down-and-out people who kept body and soul together selling door-to-door while they were looking for a job. For instance, household products, such as knives, cooking utensils, and cleaning products, are best sold at night when families are home. That leaves the daytime free for job hunting. The experience of being a salesperson is good, and it is possible to earn very good money.

(*The Direct Selling Directory*) lists specialty sales firms who need door-to-door salesmen. It is published annually by the magazine *Specialty Salesman.*[19] *Salesman's Opportunity Magazine*[20] also publishes a directory issue.)

Taking a temporary job working for an employment contractor (look under Employment Contractors–Temporary Employment in the Yellow Pages) can be a good way to earn and learn while you are looking for a full-time job. Smart students who are still in college do this kind of work during the summer not only to make money but also to have the chance to observe all kinds of work and organizations from the inside and pick up various kinds of experience.

Not infrequently, people end up with a full-time job as the result of a temporary assignment, like the fellow who was "rented" to an organization that was putting its records onto a computer. The job was keypunching—ordinary clerical work—but kinks developed in the computer system and he got involved in straightening them out. "As a result," he explained, "I got to know both the old manual system and the new computerized system. The company's management didn't want to put all its eggs in the computer system right away and wanted to keep some aspects of the old system in operation for a while. The old-timers didn't understand the computer system, and the computer people didn't understand the old system, and as someone who had worked in between, I knew them both. The company asked me to stay on for a while full time, then made the job permanent."

IX. The Sideways Strategy

This story pertains to someone who wanted a management job but was actually already a manager. "When I got out of college," he told me, "I wanted to get into a management training program with some large company, but I didn't get anywhere with college recruiters. Then back home, the Main Street employers wanted someone with experience.

"From my summer job experiences, I knew that the one place in which it was easy to get a job was the fast-food industry. The turnover is terrific. If you stick around, the first thing you know, you're an assistant manager. It's a demanding job, but you have a title. I did a good job as an assistant manager and kept pressing the main company to give me my own restaurant to manage. The company kept promising me it would, but nothing came through. Then another fast-food outfit offered me a job as manager of one of its smaller restaurants. I took the job and was soon promoted to be manager of a larger one. Later, the company made me a district manager, supervising the managers of five restaurants.

"Even though the hours are wicked and the pay isn't great, I am sure I could move up in the organization, but I would rather move into the field of financial management. For this I need accounting courses, and my present job involves too much traveling to allow me to go to school at night. To sum it up, I want to use my experience as a retail manager to help me sell myself to a firm where I can get training in another management field."

He got many job offers, once he learned to convince employers that his management skills could be used in another field besides fast food.

X. Serendipity

The two of them were totally attuned to the meritocracy and the professions. They believed that the way to get ahead in the world was to get an advanced degree and qualify for a professional position. He had his Ph.D. in economics and an offer to join the economics department of a major bank; her degree was an M.S. in student personnel, but as yet she had been unable to find a job. Since the job he had lined up was in a metropolitan area with many colleges, they decided that he should take the job; surely sooner or later there would be an opening for someone with her excellent credentials.

The decision required moving. The wife was the one who did most of the looking for a house in their new community, mostly with a particular real estate agent whom she found especially likable. The agent was a woman like herself who had also hoped to go to work for an organization but had decided to try real estate when nothing else came along. The germ of an idea was planted in the wife's mind.

When she was unable to find a job immediately, her natural inclination was to return to college and get still another degree. A career in law appealed to her. She was very ambitious, and a law degree would put her on the track to the success she sought, but the idea of selling real estate stuck in her mind. It wasn't her notion of a profession, yet she had enjoyed their own search for a home. Why not give it a try if she could get an agency to take her on? It was already October, and she wouldn't be able to enter law school until the following September anyway.

In her first year in real estate, she earned $40,000 and had a ball. She never looked back—and never did go back for that extra degree.

Notes

1. Alexis de Tocqueville, *Democracy in America*, vol. 2, revised by Francis Bowen, edited by Phillips Bradley (New York: Vintage Books, Random House, 1945). Copyright 1945 by Alfred A. Knopf, Inc.
2. Daniel Melcher, *Book Publishing* (New York: Publishers Weekly). Pamphlet, out of print.
3. *CPC Annual* (Bethlehem, Pa.: College Placement Council, Inc.). Annual.
4. Malcolm Forbes, *How to Write a Business Letter* (Elmsford, N.Y.: International Paper Co., 1979). Handout and advertisement.
5. Christopher Billy, ed., *Engineering, Science, and Computer Jobs* (Princeton, N.J.: Peterson's Guides). Annual.
6. Bernard Klein, ed., *Guide to American Directories*, 11th ed. (Coral Springs, Fla.: B. Klein Publications, 1982).
7. James M. Ethridge, ed., *The Directory of Directories*, 3rd ed. (Detroit: Gale Research, 1984).
8. *Encyclopedia of Associations*, 19th ed., vol. 1, *National Organizations of the United States* (Detroit: Gale Research, 1980).
9. *The Working Press of the Nation*, vol. 2, *Magazine and Editorial Directory* (Chicago: National Research Bureau). Annual, January.
10. *Encyclopedia of Associations*, op. cit.
11. *National Trade and Professional Associations* (Washington, D.C.: Columbia Books). Annual, January.
12. Rockcastle, Madeline T., *Where to Start: An Annotated Career Planning Bibliography* (Princeton, N.J.: Peterson's Guides, 1985).
13. Klein, op. cit.
14. Mel London, *Getting into Film* (New York: Ballantine Books, 1979).
15. Archie M. Palmer, ed., *Research Centers Directory*, 6th ed. (Detroit: Gale Research, 1979).
16. *Industrial Research Laboratories of the United States*, 15th and 16th eds. (New York: R. R. Bowker, 1977 and 1979).
17. *The Working Press of the Nation*, vol. 2, op. cit.
18. *The Working Press of the Nation*, vol. 5, *Internal Publications Directory* (Chicago: National Research Bureau). Annual, January.
19. *Specialty Salesman and Business Opportunity*, 307 North Michigan Avenue, Chicago, Illinois 60601.
20. *Salesman's Opportunity Magazine*, 6 North Michigan Avenue, Suite 1405, Chicago, Illinois 60602.

21. Figler, Howard, *The Complete Job-Search Handbook* (New York: Holt, Rinehart and Winston, 1979).
22. Bolles, Richard N., *What Color Is Your Parachute?* (Berkeley, Calif.: The Ten Speed Press, 1985).
23. Bureau of Labor Statistics, *Occupational Outlook Handbook* (Washington, D.C.: U.S. Government Printing Office, 1984–85).
24. Christopher Billy, ed., *Business and Management Jobs* (Princeton, N.J.: Peterson's Guides). Annual.

Comments Relating to Bibliography

Since I have harped on the importance of literature research in the conduct of a career exploration and a job search, and since what is probably the best career library in the country was developed during my tenure as Director of Cornell's Career Center, it may seem strange that I have not included an extensive bibliography with this book. Probably because I have been involved in the publication of *Where to Start: An Annotated Career Planning Bibliography*, I know what a bibliography should be.

Even if this book were three times its present size I couldn't begin to match *Where to Start*, and if I included anything less, I might give the impression that I had sorted through the literature and selected the most important. I have noted publications in the text, and good ones I think, but they were mentioned primarily to illustrate the uses of books and other publications in job hunting. Books are indispensable resources and the indispensable guide to them is *Where to Start*. If your library does not have a copy ask your librarian to get one.

Have You Seen These Other Publications from Peterson's Guides?

Liberal Arts Power!
How to Sell It on Your Résumé
Burton Jay Nadler
This is the first résumé book written exclusively for generalists, liberal arts students, recent graduates, and career changers. Using about 30 sample résumés, the author shows job hunters how to define their skills in terms of the jobs they want.

8½" x 11", 118 pages Stock no. 2545
ISBN 0-87866-254-5 **$6.95** paperback

Where to Start:
An Annotated Career-planning Bibliography
FIFTH EDITION, 1985–87
Madeline T. Rockcastle
This book is published by Cornell University's Career Center, which houses one of the best career libraries in the nation, and describes the career-planning publications used there. It covers books, periodicals, audiovisual resources, and other materials and is an invaluable tool for human resource managers, counselors, and librarians in both corporate and academic organizations.

8½" x 11", 278 pages Stock no. 3843
ISBN 0-87866-384-3 **$12.95** paperback

Finding a Job in Your Field:
A Handbook for Ph.D.'s and M.A.'s
Rebecca Anthony and Gerald Roe
This practical and thorough guide is the only book written especially for holders of advanced degrees to explain how they should prepare for academic and professional employment. It includes an assessment of the job choices available, advice on organizing a job search, tips on how to write effective vitas and résumés, advice on how to interview with search committees, and other specific and very helpful information.

6" x 9", 144 pages Stock no. 2782
ISBN 0-87866-278-2 **$8.95** paperback

Peterson's Annual Guides/Careers
Business and Management Jobs 1986
SECOND EDITION
Editor: Christopher Billy
Data Editor: John Wells
The second edition of this distinctive career guide details hundreds of organizations that specifically recruit employees in the nontechnical areas of business and management. Gives detailed information about each organization including starting salaries and locations, benefits, training, and recent hiring patterns at the entry level. Academic disciplines currently being recruited are listed together with the likely starting assignments.

8½" x 11", 268 pages Stock no. 3495
ISBN 0-87866-349-5 **$14.95** paperback

Liberal Arts Jobs
Burton Jay Nadler
The only book to specifically describe jobs for liberal arts majors in detail. This is a comprehensive directory that goes beyond the usual overviews of career fields. Over 150 job titles in more than 50 career fields suitable for the liberal arts graduate are included, ranging from the traditional to the often-overlooked. Each description includes useful, specific information on typical job functions, appropriate skills and aptitudes, and hiring requirements—all necessary for the college-educated generalist considering a career.

8½" x 11", about 125 pages Stock no. 4432
ISBN 0-87866-443-2 **$9.95** paperback

New Horizons:
The Education and Career Planning Guide for Adults
William C. Haponski, Ph.D., and Charles E. McCabe, M.B.A.
Expert advice for the adult who is thinking of going back to school at any level. Covers choosing a program, finding financial aid, coping with pressures, and making career decisions. Originally published as *Back to School: The College Guide for Adults*, this new edition places heavier emphasis on career-related aspects of adult education.

6" x 9", 249 pages Stock no. 3304
ISBN 0-87866-330-4 **$8.95** paperback

Peterson's Annual Guides/Graduate Study
Graduate and Professional Programs:
An Overview 1986
TWENTIETH EDITION
Series Editor: Amy J. Goldstein
Data Editor: Andrea C. Frary
Covers the spectrum of U.S. and Canadian graduate programs in a single reliable volume. The organizational structure and heads at each level are shown for every institution, together with details on facilities, enrollment, faculty, and research. Includes a complete list of over 1,400 schools with all graduate and professional degrees they offer.

8½" x 11", about 900 pages Stock no. 3428
ISBN 0-87866-342-8 **$16.95** paperback

Peterson's Graduate Education Directory
Editors: Paul Miers, Ph.D., and Amy J. Goldstein

This directory is the complete guide to graduate education in the United States and Canada. It includes over 1,400 accredited institutions offering graduate degrees. Each listing has an overview describing the type of institution and giving data on number of students and tuition. There is also a roster of the top administrative officers, such as director of sponsored research and head librarian. Separate entries outline all of the graduate and professional schools at each institution and list degrees offered right down to programs within departments. Because it contains the name, title, and phone number of each administrative head, this directory is a valuable reference for anyone who deals regularly with higher education.

8½" x 11", about 750 pages   Stock no. 4459
ISBN 0-87866-445-9   **$29.95** paperback

How to Order

These publications are available from booksellers, or you may order direct from **Peterson's Guides, Dept. 6601, P.O. Box 2123, Princeton, New Jersey 08540-2123.** Please note that prices are subject to change without notice.

- Enclose full payment for each book, plus postage and handling charges as follows:

Amount of Order	4th-Class Postage and Handling Charges
$1–$10	$1.75
$10.01–$20	$2.75
$20.01–$40	$3.75
$40.01 +	Add $1.00 shipping and handling for every additional $20 worth of books ordered.

Place your order TOLL-FREE by calling 800-225-0261 between 8:30 A.M. and 4:30 P.M. Eastern time, Monday through Friday. From New Jersey, Alaska, Hawaii, and outside the United States, call 609-924-5338. Telephone orders over $15 may be charged to your charge card; institutional and trade orders over $20 may be billed.

- For faster shipment via United Parcel Service (UPS), add $2.00 over and above the appropriate fourth-class book-rate charges listed.
- Bookstores and tax-exempt organizations should contact us for appropriate discounts.
- You may charge your order to VISA, MasterCard, or American Express. Minimum charge order: $15. Please include the name, account number, and validation and expiration dates for charge orders.
- New Jersey residents should add 6% sales tax to the cost of the books, excluding the postage and handling charge.
- Write for a free catalog describing all of our latest publications.